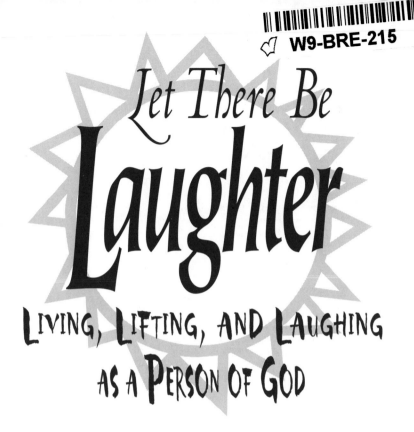

Let There Be Laughter

LIVING, LIFTING, AND LAUGHING AS A PERSON OF GOD

RICHARD W. BIMLER

ROBERT D. BIMLER

CPH

SAINT LOUIS

THiS BooK iS DEDiCATED TO ALL THoSE iN oUR FAMiLY WHo HAVE LAUGHED AT oUR JoKES AND SToRiES THRoUGHoUT THE YEARS—BoTH oF YoU!

Cover photographs: © The Stock Market (clockwise from top) Bill Miles, Mugshots, Ronnie Kaufman.

The following chapters are adapted from articles written by Rich Bimler that originally appeared in *Lutheran Education*: 10, 13, 16, 25, 26, 41. Reprinted with permission.

The following chapters are adapted from articles written by Rich Bimler that originally appeared in *Good Shepherd*: 24, 31, 37. Reprinted with permission.

The following chapters are adapted from articles written by Rich Bimler that originally appeared in *Family Talk*: 36, 38. Reprinted with permission.

The following chapter is adapted from the article "Shaping the Future," written by Rich Bimler, which originally appeared in Volume 2, Issue 1 of *Lutheran Education Association*: 11. Reprinted with permission.

All Scripture quotations, unless otherwise indicated, are taken from the HOLY BIBLE, NEW INTERNATIONAL VERSION®. NIV®. Copyright © 1973, 1978, 1984 by International Bible Society. Used by permission of Zondervan Publishing House. All rights reserved.

Scripture quotations marked TEV are from the Good News Bible, the Bible in TODAY'S ENGLISH VERSION. Copyright © American Bible Society, 1966, 1971, 1976. Used by permission.

Library of Congress Cataloging-in-Publication Data
Bimler, Richard.
   Let there be laughter: living, lifting, and laughing as a person of God / Richard W. and Robert D. Bimler
   p.   cm.   ISBN 0-570-05356-0
   1. Meditations. 2. Christian life—humor.
   I. Bimler Robert D.   II. Title.
BV4832.2.B493   1999
242–dc21   99-20570

1 2 3 4 5 6 7 8 9 10   08   07 06 05 04 03 02 01 00 99

CONTENTS OF CELEBRATION!

Introduction 5

1 What This Book Can Do for You 7
2 Holy Hilarity 9
3 Health, Hope, and Humor! 11
4 Let There Be Laughter in the Scriptures—Ta-da! 14
5 Psalm 126:3 15
6 Hope and Hooray 17
7 How Friendly Is Your Congregation? 18
8 Laughing at Life, Laughing at Death 21
9 Honest Hymns 23
10 Checking Up 25
11 "Laugh, Then, Wherever You May Be!" 28
12 Top 10 List of How to Live, Lift, and Laugh
    as a Person of God 33
13 The Little Girl Who Couldn't Smile 36
14 Growing Old—Gratefully 39
15 Laughing at and During Meetings 42
16 How Do You Spell C-E-L-E-B-R-A-T-E? 44
17 Listening to the Sounds of Kids 47
18 "Down Under," Down Under 49
19 I Can Only Please One Person 51
20 Don't Let the Kids Have All the Fun! 52
21 Letter from Camp 55
22 To Play and to Pray 58
23 I've Got the Joy, Joy, Joy 60
24 Top 10 List of How to Keep Happy and Healthy
    as a Family of God! 62
25 I Am Special! (I Really Am!) 67

26 Do Be Do Be Do! 70
27 Theology of T-shirts 73
28 To Celebrate Life Means to Share Life 75
29 Chain Laughter 77
30 The Good Fridays and Easters of Our Lives 78
31 Life Is For-Giving! 80
32 Laughter—An Encouraging Sign
    of the Presence of God 85
33 Where Has All the Laughter Gone? 87
34 Things to Do for Fun at Home 89
35 Laugh, Even Though It Hurts 93
36 Humorous Family Vacations or
    It Didn't Seem Funny at the Time! 95
37 Ho-Ho-Home Is Where the Har-Har-Heart Is! 99
38 Grandparenting Is "Grand"! 105
39 I Can't See the Dark! 108
40 What's Taken So Long? 110
41 I Wish I Had Said That! 112
42 Affirming Those around Us 116
43 Just for Fun 118
44 Easter Joy Turns the World Upside Down! 121
45 Time Is Celebration 123
46 The Gift of Today 125
47 Rise ... and Whine! 127
48 Jesus Is with Us 129
49 Celebrating Life 131
50 A Quiet Joy 133
51 Children and Adults—Together 134
52 Guidelines for Celebrating the Christ-Life 136
53 Well Now! 137
54 A Final Word on—Let There Be Laughter! 138

Sarah's Christmas Scenario—1998 139
12 Warning Signs of Health 143
Endnotes 144

iNTRODUCTioN

Let There Be Laughter! What a wonderful affirmation of our faith in the Lord.

God calls each of us to be a light, a hope, a promise of His presence in our lives. We share our lives, our dreams, and ourselves with those around us. And as we walk and talk our faith, we bring a celebrative lifestyle to others because we know what life in Christ Jesus is all about. What's more, we know how it all will turn out. Christ is alive! He has risen for each of us. In taking away the fear of dying, Christ has also taken away the fear of living!

So, let there be laughter! If people of God are not able to laugh in this life, who is? We can and do laugh and celebrate because Christ has already done everything for us to assure us of life eternal—and life in Him every day. Now that really is something to celebrate!

This book is a father and son effort. More accurately, it could be called a father, son, with lots of help from the Holy Spirit effort!

Rich, the father, and Bob, the son, have shared joys, tears, struggles, and laughter and have attempted to help each other focus on the fact that we are called to "let there be laughter" in all that we do. In the following pages we hope to share some of our laughter with you. And as we share our hopes and joys and struggles and stories with you, we hope and pray that this will entice you to do the same with those around you.

This is not a joke book nor is it a book that encourages you to "whistle a happy tune" and "don't worry—be happy."

Instead, it is a resource that seriously encourages you to focus first of all on the fact that God loves us in Christ Jesus and forgives and frees us to be His celebrating people in our daily lives. It is a book that exclaims loudly and boldly, and hopefully humorously, the fact that we need the Lord Jesus in our daily lives to celebrate life as holy and as a gift from God.

May these pages bring many joy-filled thoughts and feelings to you and encourage you to tell and live your stories of Good Friday and Easter!

May the power of the Spirit tickle you each day!

Let there be laughter—in Christ Jesus!

Rich Bimler—the father

Bob Bimler—the son

(With lots of help from the Holy Spirit)

1

WHAT THIS BOOK CAN DO FOR YOU

The authors hope and pray this resource will enlighten your lives and will affirm in you the faith that is ours in Christ Jesus! These pages will continue to point you to the cross and the resurrection as the source of all of our joy and celebration.

Watch for these words and ideas to

1 Help you celebrate your faith in Christ Jesus—right now, today.

2 Enable you to laugh and celebrate life with those around you.

3 Provide a positive mind-set for you, grounded in your faith in the Lord.

4 Help you to smile and not to take yourself toooo seriously!

5 Provide you with some good stories and anecdotes to share with your serious and grouchy friends.

6 Encourage you to tell your stories of faith and life to others. (And write them down for others to read!)

7 Motivate you to bring joy and laughter into other people's lives.

7

8	Cause you to celebrate the big and little things in life.
9	Help you to live out a life full of health and hope in the name of the healing Christ.
10	Nudge you to enjoy yourself and help others to enjoy themselves as well.

Watch for the little "joys" all around you in life. Throughout these pages, you will find scattered a good dose of little sayings, questions, and other statements. Read them, laugh or groan, then move on to the main content of the stories and chapters.

And as you see and read these little "ditties," hopefully they will help you to be more aware of the little "surprises" that are all around us in our daily lives—the little things kids say, the weird bumper sticker on the car in front of you, the sign in the store, the conversation overheard at the watercooler, the wise words of your elderly friend. Watch for these surprises in your life … and celebrate them too!

Now, on to the stories and anecdotes and celebration of life to the fullest—in Christ Jesus. Enjoy the reading, share your stories, make these better, and above all, continue to affirm in each other that our Lord, Jesus Christ, is very much alive and well in the experiences of His people of faith—you and me.

Happy reading!
Happy celebrating!
Happy holy laughter!

Should vegetarians eat animal crackers?

2

HOLY HILARITY

Laughter is an example of "holy hilarity."

For us Webster-lovers, we know that "holy" means "to be set apart for a special purpose." Mr. Webster, whose wife, during conversations, could not get even a word in edgewise, defines "hilarity" as "boisterous merriment"!

Holy hilarity, then, is affirmation of the fact that God gives us a life to live—and live to the fullest (John 10:10). He wants us to see our life as "set apart" from the standards of the world so we can celebrate the joy of the Easter resurrection with those around us.

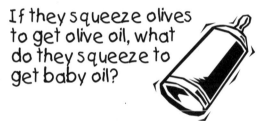

If they squeeze olives to get olive oil, what do they squeeze to get baby oil?

I remember many years ago at Trinity, in Mission, Kansas, when we celebrated Easter by putting balloons throughout the church. For many, it was a positive visible sign of the resurrection and joy in the Lord. For some, it came off as too secular and worldly. But for the authors, it pointed out the fact that there really are balloons of joy and resurrection in our lives each day as the Spirit gives us power and hope. We just don't see them! Many times the problem is that we are so involved in the struggles of our Good Fridays that we fail to notice those Easter balloons flying all around us.

Holy hilarity is about seeing those balloons soaring and bringing the power of the Spirit to us each and every day. It's about celebrating our faith in the Lord Jesus Christ. It's about realizing that people of God live on "this side of the resurrection." It's about dealing with the hurts of our Good Fridays because we know in faith about the hoorays of our Easters, in Christ Jesus.

So enjoy, laugh, reflect, share, and especially celebrate the "holy hilarity" that the Lord gives to us as a gift each day. Celebrate and affirm the fact that we are indeed set apart to live life to the fullest, as we laugh with the Lord because of what He has done for us!

Why don't they make the entire airplane out of what they use for the "indestructible black box"?

HEALTH, HOPE, AND HUMOR!

A word about health, hope, and humor, in the name of the healing Christ.

Humor is a healing gift from the Lord. To laugh means to surrender our lives to our Lord, to say, "Lord, I'm in trouble without You. Please help me!" Laughter moves us away from ourselves and focuses our lives on the Lord and on others. Laughter is of great spiritual value because it "self-distances" us. Laughter allows us to take our eyes off ourselves.

This kind of laughter and humor is not necessarily the kind we see alive and well in society. Humor can be misused, like all other gifts. But humor and laughter that is focused in Christ points us to the cross and the resurrection. It shows how really human we are and how lost in sin we are without the saving action of Jesus Christ.

Life is about staggering onward, rejoicing in the Lord. The power of the Spirit allows us to see life as a gift, despite our shortcomings and problems, because we view life through the cross and the resurrection.

This resource is not only about laughter and humor, but also about health and hope in the name of the healing Christ. Health and healing are salvation words. Often salvation is seen as "other worldly only," as something that happens after this life, which has nothing to do with the here and now. But salvation in Christ is about human wholeness and about celebrating that wholeness in Christ with others. Christ reestablished this wholeness that was broken, disrupted, and disintegrated. The Gospel promises healing and health right now, in Christ. We are not saved because we celebrate life and can laugh out loud, but we celebrate and can laugh out loud because we are saved in Christ Jesus! Where two or three are gathered in Christ, it's the time and place for a celebration.

Why do parents yell at their children, and then ask, "Did you hear me?"

CORE VALUES

Wheat Ridge Ministries is an independent organization committed to seeding new ministries of health and hope in the name of the healing Christ. It has developed a system of "core values" by which to live and minister. These focus on basic Christian values that are lived out each day in our lives. Individuals also have core values, spoken or unspoken, that reveal what is important in life. Try these.

1   LOOK—to the Lord and His Church. Focus life through Word and Sacrament.

2   LISTEN—to the people around you. See their gifts, their needs, their ups, their downs.

3   LIFT—Affirm people, encourage them in the Lord. Build up, support them.

4   LINK—Connect people with people, ideas with ideas, needs with gifts. Celebrate the Holy Huddle, the church, by bringing people together in faith and ministry.

5   LEARN—from each other, be global thinkers; use your gifts, share your life with others.

6   LAUGH—Celebrate and enjoy life with others. Celebrate our one faith in the Lord of hope and healing.

As we apply these core values by living a holy life of hilarity, we begin to see life as an everyday celebration. And we see how laughter and joy encompass all of life as we give thanks to the Lord, "for He is good"!

LET THERE BE LAUGHTER IN THE SCRIPTURES —TA-DA!

There are more than 800 passages in the Bible that deal with "joy." God must be serious about celebrating life!

There is a story of a little boy who came home from Sunday school on Easter Sunday very excited about what he had learned. He raced into the kitchen and shouted, "Wow, I learned what Jesus said when He burst out of the tomb on Easter morning!" His mom and dad were excited too, and they asked him, "Well, what did He say on that first Easter morning?" And the little boy ran up to them, threw his hands up in the air, and said, "TA-DA!"

Now that probably was a loose translation, but the little boy certainly captured the essence of joy and celebration in the Lord.

And we, too, live TA-DA! lives because of that first Easter morning.

Have a TA-DA! day in the Lord!

There is a tongue depressor, but is there anything to cheer a tongue up?

PSALM 126:3

THE LORD HAS DONE GREAT THINGS FOR US!

Psalm 126:3 says it all: "The LORD has done great things for us, and we are filled with joy." Wow, talk about a mission statement! The psalmist zeroes in on the fact that it is God Himself who is the Giver of all of life and our response is a life filled with joy.

Often, at least for me, the joy is lost in my worrying about what I didn't do well or should have done better. Instead of being filled with joy, I am filled with worry or anxiety or even fear. But the Spirit continues to point all of us back to the cross and 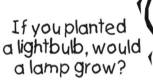 the resurrection so we see once again, each day, that the Lord has done it all for us. He loves and forgives us even when our lives are not filled with joy. And this is what brings us joy—the forgiveness we have in Christ. Talk about great things the Lord has done!

The theme of one women's auxiliary organization affiliated with the church is, "Serve the Lord with

If you planted a lightbulb, would a lamp grow?

gladness." Unfortunately in everyday life this sometimes comes out, "Serve the Lord with sadness" when
we get caught up in our own foibles and problems.
Ministry can become negative, tedious, problem-
focused, and full of sadness. But what you and I can
celebrate each day is the fact that the Lord comes to
us and takes the sadness of our lives and turns it into
gladness, in Him, through the power of the Spirit
working through us. What a gift. What a reason for
joy and laughter!

Our role as joy-filled people of God is to take the
gladnesses of our lives and intersect them with the
sadnesses of others' lives. It helps to connect laughter
and celebration with the powerful ministry we all
have of bringing joy in the Lord to those who do not
yet know that joy.

What's another word
for "thesaurus"?

HOPE AND HOORAY

Scripture is full of exciting messages of health and hope. One of the most important of these messages is "new every day." God's Word comes to us in the midst of our joys and sorrows, and familiar words take on new meaning each day because of our new experiences in life, new experiences that give us new reason for celebration.

Listen to Isaiah 55:12: "You will go out in joy and be led forth in peace; the mountains and hills will burst into song before you, and all the trees of the field will clap their hands."

Have you ever heard mountains singing? Have you seen those trees clapping? Have they seen and heard you clapping and singing?

If you have, continue the celebration each day. If you have not yet heard that noise and seen that action, watch for it the next time you are outside in God's creation. Through the eyes of the cross and the resurrection of Christ, all things are alive in the Lord.

And talk about hope in the Lord— listen to this blessing from Romans 15:13: "May the God of hope fill you with all joy and peace as you trust in Him, so that you may overflow with hope by the power of the Holy Spirit."

Hooray for hope—in the Lord!

Do shy turtles ever come out of their shells?

7

HoW FRiENDLY iS YOUR CONGREGATioN?

How friendly is your congregation—really? Not among those you already know, but around those you do not know. Are visitors and new members made to feel welcome and a part of your spiritual community?

One of the many "Top 10" lists out these days shares a number of ways you can gauge if your church is friendly, such as:

* The choir begins to sing—and can't stop!

* As the pastor ends his sermon, the people chant, "We want more! We want more!"

* The ushers rush up to the pastor at the end of the service and douse him with a cooler of Gatorade!

What are some other ways that announce to people that you and your church are friendly and happy to see new faces? Too often, at least in congregations I've observed, it is easy to gather and visit only with those people you already know and leave the new folks standing alone. I don't think that is what Martin Luther had in mind when he said, "Here I stand!"

When we were in Australia last year, we experienced a friendly congregation that had a very effective plan of action for visitors. After the service, the pastor announced that the "three-minute rule" was in effect. He explained that the three-minute rule was this: For the first three minutes after the service had concluded, no members could talk to other members of the congregation—they had to focus on introducing themselves to the visitors.

I also remember visiting another congregation a few years ago. After the service, I was standing in the entryway, talking to no one. Of course, I was a visitor! I thought I would be proactive so I approached an elderly gentleman who seemed alone and possibly a visitor also. I asked a very ill-conceived question of him. "Are you a visitor too?"

He stared at me, then said sternly, "Of course not, I've been a member for 19 years."

What do you give a sick chicken, people soup?!

The clincher came when he added, "And I was even a greeter last week!"

This man served as a "friendly" greeter last week, so he doesn't have to be friendly for the next six weeks—until he is a greeter again.

Continue to celebrate the best reason of all to be friendly—the joy and love given to us in Christ. Continue to celebrate the positive relationships that have developed in your congregation. Look for ways

Would not-so-happy
people only be
on cloud 3?!

to enhance the friend-liness of your Holy Huddle, the church. And pray that the Lord continues to pro-vide people of all ages, shapes, colors, and sizes to your congrega-tion so the Spirit can work in and through all of you.

Next Sunday, why not invite someone to join you for worship—and even let them sit in your own, personal pew?

LAUGHING AT LIFE, LAUGHING AT DEATH

Where, O death, is your victory?
Where, O death, is your sting? 1 Corinthians 15:55

We live on "this side" of the resurrection. We know how things turn out. We are victorious in life and in death because of what Christ Jesus has done for us. This is what we celebrate!

So often we continue to shy away from talking about death. We still try to hide it, to massage it, to speak vaguely about it. In devotion time this morning, I heard a lady pray for a woman who had "lost" her husband. I immediately had visions of someone getting lost in a big shopping mall.

But Scripture talks differently about death. St. Paul exclaims that the sting is gone; Christ has won the battle. All we need do is look forward to the resurrection. What a far cry from the world's idea of denying the existence of death itself.

A grandchild shared the following death notice with me recently. He did not intend to mock death or make fun of anything living or dead; he just thought it was a cute and funny story. I agree. These kind of stories can help us think about and even discuss these "serious" issues in creative and even celebrative ways.

Pillsbury Dough Boy Dead at 71

Veteran Pillsbury spokesman, Pop N. Fresh, died yesterday of a severe yeast infection. He was 71. Fresh was buried in one of the largest funeral ceremonies in recent years. Dozens of celebrities turned out, including Mrs. Butterworth, the California Raisins, Hungry Jack, Betty Crocker, and the Hostess Twinkies. Betty sang "When the Roll Is Called Up Yonder."

The graveside was piled high with flours as longtime friend Aunt Jemima delivered the eulogy, describing Fresh as a man who "never knew how much he was kneaded."

Fresh rose quickly in show business, but his later life was filled with many turnovers. He was not considered a very smart cookie, wasting much of his dough on half-baked schemes. Still, even as a crusty old man, he was a roll model for millions.

Fresh is survived by his second wife. They have two children and one in the oven. The funeral was held at 4:50 for about 20 minutes.

Author Unknown

If the funeral procession is at night, do folks drive with their lights off?

22

HONEST HYMNS

Have you ever played with the idea of how some of our good Christian hymns would be sung if we were really honest about how we feel? Because of our sin, we often fail to keep our commitment to the Lord, and we waver at how dedicated we really are to Him and His Church.

Maybe, then, it is a good thing that our hymnbooks do not list some of the following make-believe hymns:

* "Take My Life and Let Me Be"
* "Onward, Christian Reserves"
* "I Surrender Some"
* "Oh, How I Like Jesus"
* "He's Quite a Bit to Me"
* "I Love to Talk about Telling the Story"
* "Here Am I, Send Him"
* "Where He Leads Me, I Will Consider Following"
* "Just as I Pretend to Be"

and my all-time favorite,

* "When the Saints Go Sneaking In"

We thank the Lord that He is a loving and forgiving Lord who loves us constantly, even though we sometimes get our priorities and commitments messed up. And we thank the Lord for His total commitment to us. He can be trusted, even when we do not keep our trust in Him. And we can be bold to deal head-on with our selfishness and misdirected lives because of what God has done for us in Christ Jesus.

Does skim milk come from anorexic cows?

10

CHECKiNG UP

How's your health?

If you and I want to be influences on the health and fitness of those we love and serve, we need to first take care of ourselves. There is a compelling influence in the power of personal example that will ripple outward to our family, our co-workers, our congregation. Yes, health is certainly more infectious than disease!

Here are 12 "warning signs" to check out your health level.

1   A strong presence of a "friendly flock," a "holy huddle" in your life. We need support people around us. They keep us focused, encouraged, and give us hope.

2   Chronic positive expectations—a tendency to frame events in a constructive light. Healthy people emphasize the positive and see the Lord alive each day in their lives.

3   Regular signs of joy in living. Remember Martin Luther's statement: "God is not a God

of sadness, but the devil is. Christ is a God of joy. It is pleasing to the dear God whenever you rejoice or laugh from the bottom of your heart."

4 A sense of spiritual renewal. This comes through regular opportunities for worship and study of the Scriptures, as well as a close connection with the community of saints.

5 Increased sensitivity to others. Healthy people tend to listen to others and stay sensitive to the hurts and hoorays of those around them.

6 Tendency to adapt to changing conditions. Change happens! It's all around us. Healthy people deal with change realistically and positively.

7 Increased appetite for physical activity. Run, walk, stretch—30 minutes a day can really keep the doctor away!

8 Tendency to identify and communicate feelings. Healthy people are able to express themselves and deal with their own struggles and joys by sharing with others.

9 Repeated episodes of gratitude, generosity, and hope. Healthy people tend to be thankful people and people who give of themselves to others.

10 Compulsion to care for other people. We move from our own self-centeredness to a life of others-centeredness.

11 Persistent sense of humor. Healthy people can laugh at themselves—out loud! We can see the humor in our failings and our mistakes, which continue to point us to the Lord. Remember, "Laughter is another way of crossing oneself."

12 Lives in the forgiveness of Christ! We are forgiven! That's something to celebrate and to share!

What are other signs in your life and in the lives of those around you of health and hope? Watch for these signs, encourage them in others, and share your life of hope with family, congregation, and in your various communities.

Healthy living is contagious—let's pray for an epidemic!

Why is it called "rush hour" when nobody's moving?

11

"LAUGH, THEN, WHEREVER YOU MAY BE!"

To paraphrase a popular Christian song, "Laugh, then, wherever you may be, for I am the Lord of the laugh, said He." Yes, we can laugh and dance through life because we are living on this side of the resurrection! Through all the Good Fridays in our lives, we know that the Lord continues to give us His Easters. And because of this, we can help keep ourselves and those around us focused on the Lord, who allows us to dance and laugh through life.

During one of his many talkative moods, Martin Luther connected physical and mental health by pointing out that "our physical health depends in large measure on the thoughts of our minds." More and more recent studies make the connection between being able to laugh at ourselves and keeping ourselves healthy. Now laughing in itself will not keep disease away, but laughing and a positive outlook on life, through Jesus Christ, allows us to sense and see the Spirit soaring through our lives each day.

Studies also point out the psychological benefits of laughter. For example, laughter

1. Relieves tension and stress.
2. Provides a new perspective.
3. Helps keep us balanced.
4. Helps us cope.
5. Gives us empowerment.
6. Makes us feel good.
7. Makes others wonder what we are thinking.

Isn't it a bit unnerving that doctors call what they do "practice"?!

There are also physical benefits. Laughter

1. Increases antibodies to fight respiratory infections.
2. Secretes enzymes to protect the stomach from forming ulcers.
3. Conditions abdominal muscles.
4. Relaxes muscles throughout the body.
5. Reduces blood pressure and heart rate.
6. Releases endorphins for natural pain relief.
7. Moves nutrients and oxygen to body tissues.
8. Increases alertness.
9. Makes us feel good.
10. Points us to the fact that God is still in control.

A good experiment is shared in *Don't Get Mad, Get Funny* by Leigh Ann Jasheway[1] and *The Healing Power of Humor* by Allen Klein[2]. They point out that we should use a stress index to deal with stress situations in our lives. Try it out. List an event or circumstance that was stressful for you and the date it happened. Then chart the date you were able to laugh about the situation and how you found the humor in that particular circumstance. There may be situations you never find humorous, but being conscious of this index can help you become more aware of using humor in your daily life. It's worth a try. It might even be worth a laugh!

Have you ever seen deer and antelope playing?

Another study, done by the University of Michigan, points out that the average elementary school child (whoever that is) smiles and laughs 150 times a day. The "average" adult smiles and laughs 15 times a day. Now you may think that sounds high for the average adult you know, but it is interesting that the older we get, the less we laugh and enjoy life. Like our friend Martin once said, "People don't stop laughing because they grow old, they grow old because they stop laughing."

The whole point of "laughing at life" is that we surrender our lives to the Lord. It means we can say to ourselves, "Hey, we're in trouble without You, Lord. Fill us with Your Spirit and help us celebrate life."

Here are some suggestions for you and me about how we can live out a positive, emotional life in the Lord through joy and laughter.

1 Give yourself permission to laugh. It's okay! And it gives others permission to laugh at themselves as well.

2 Share your joys, your sorrows, your highs, your lows, and even your "ho hums" with others around you.

3 Hug someone daily. (You should probably know the person first!)

4 Be a good listener for others. Don't be like the 85-year-old lady who, when her family wanted her to get a hearing aid, simply said, "I don't need one. At 85, I've heard everything I want to hear!"

5 Think positive thoughts. Keep focused on the joys and the hope of the Lord in you.

6 Remember who you are and whose you are. Rejoice in your Baptism!

7 Spend time with friendly people. Sure, we need to be sensitive to the "grouches" in our lives, but we also need to be built up and affirmed by the "friendly flock" of God's people around us.

8 Deal honestly and specifically with your feelings. We spend a lot of time with ourselves, so it's best to get to know ourselves as honestly as possible.

9 Give yourself a break. Forgive yourself for past messes. God already has! And live each day the way the Lord intends for us to live—as forgiven, free, and festive folks!

10 Continue to develop your care-giving skills. Reach out with love and laughter to those around you. Keep people in ministry range with one another.

By laughing and celebrating the life of Christ in us, we allow others to see the presence of the Lord working in and through us. Thus, we can pray the Clowns' Prayer: "Lord, as I stumble through this life, help me to create more laughter than tears, dispense more happiness than gloom, spread more cheer than despair. Never let me become so indifferent that I will fail to see the wonder in the eyes of a child or the twinkle in the eyes of the aged … and, Lord, in my final moment, may I hear Your whisper, 'When you made My people smile, you made Me smile.'"

So let's continue to "laugh, then, wherever we may be, for I am the Lord of the laugh, said He." And while we're laughing, let's dance a little too!

If two candles are dating, should you say that they're going out together?

12

TOP 10 LIST
OF HOW TO LIVE, LIFT, AND LAUGH AS A PERSON OF GOD

10 Lighten up! If you love Jesus, why don't you tell your face about it? Christ is the Light of the world, and that makes us lights also, even when we don't look like it or act like it or feel like it. "Lighten up!" is not a mandate; it is an affirmation of who we are in Christ Jesus!

9 Laugh at yourself—before someone else does. The secret to laughter is to laugh at yourself, not at others. And we have so much to laugh at. People who laugh, last! It is a way of surrendering yourself to the Lord.

8 Give others permission to laugh. We need to help free people up to laugh and smile and enjoy life. They can get stuck on the "serious button" too long. For instance, once after speaking at a congregation, I was walking out and saw this very serious usher heading right for me. *Oh, oh, now what did I do?* He looked at me, seriously of course, and said, "You know, one of the stories you told almost made me smile."

7 Hang around happy people. It's fun to be around people, especially happy ones. Keep your spirits up by spending most of your time with positive, happy people. This is not to suggest that you avoid grouchy people all the time, but that you make sure you are regularly rubbing ministry shoulders with those who are celebrating their life and faith in the Lord. In doing this, you will be better prepared to deal with those more serious folks.

If the #2 pencil is
the most popular,
why is it still #2?

6 Take care of yourself. It is hard to share the joy of the Lord when we don't feel very affirming about ourselves. We need time to take care of our own bodies. Rest, a balanced diet, and regular exercise are all a part of keeping happy and healthy in the Lord. He has given us one body to use and to share and to take care of so we can be in ministry to and with others.

5 Share your life with others. Go out of your way to share your stories, your ups and downs, your

highs and lows, with others. We need each other, which is why God put us into a community called the church. Take advantage of all of those gifts of the people around you.

4 Encourage one another. There are too many discouraging things about life without us becoming one of them! Encourage, affirm, support through hugs and words and actions. And don't let those deer and antelope hear one discouraging word!

3 Tell your story of faith. We often sing, "I love to tell the story"; let's practice telling our faith stories even more than we sing them. People of all ages need to hear the Gospel message of Christ in our own words and through our own experiences.

2 Enjoy the little things in life. Forget the big things; focus on the little things that are also gifts from the Lord, like the flowers, the chirping birds, the cute talk of infants, the sounds of the city, the lights of the stars, the fun in the playground, the business of ants, the buzzing of alarm clocks, the beeping of horns. All these come to us, compliments of the Giver, as gifts. It just depends on how we will accept them, use them, and share them.

1 See all of life as a gift! "Yesterday is history, tomorrow is mystery, today is a gift—that's why we call it the present!" We celebrate today because that's all we have at this point in our lives. Today is a gift because it is God's way of coming to us with His love and forgiveness in Christ. Celebrate today, in Christ!

THE LiTTLE GiRL WHO COULDN'T SMiLE

Perhaps you remember the story from a few years ago about a 7-year-old girl in the Los Angeles area who was having surgery to repair some nerves so she would be able to smile. For all seven years of her young life, she had been unable to smile because of this condition. What a sad tale of a person who had been unable to share her feelings and joys in a way that so many of us take for granted. But we hope and pray that the surgery went well and that now she is able to smile at the world around her.

Why is the alphabet
in that order?
Is it because of
that song?!

As I thought more about this little one, it also struck me that it is a sad commentary that so many of us who have the correctly functioning nerves in our faces fail to use the gift of smiling as often as we can. I remember the sneer I made at the rude motorist who almost forced me off the road. Or the non-smiley approach I give to telemarketers who call. They can't see my face, but they can probably figure out that I'm not smiling. Or the times when I forget to use the simple gift of a smile with members of my own family or staff.

In a sense, the Lord "operated" on all of us when He came into the world to be born, live, suffer, die, and rise again. He continues to turn the frowns of sin into the festivities of freedom. He changes our Good Fridays into Easters!

The little girl who couldn't smile really has a message for us. She has no doubt brought much joy and smiles to her parents and other loved ones around her, even though she was not able to physically give a smile back to them. And each of us is called to bring health and hope and happiness to the people God puts into our lives—even today!

It's an old saying, but it still works, "If you see a person without a smile, give him one of yours!" God has given us many ways to share the joy and faith we receive each day as a gift; smiling is one of them. It affirms the fact that the Spirit continues to give new life and new hope to us, even in the midst of the "frowns" of life.

Why not try this experiment: Take a good look at yourself in the mirror. Smile. Give yourself a big smile, a little smile—even a face-stretching grin. (Perhaps this is best done when you are all alone in your private bathroom!) Practice smiling at yourself in the mirror every day and see how you look to others. Not bad! Now go out and do it in the world. Use this same smile as you go about your ministries for the next week. Flash it to your neighbors, at work, to your family, and even to that rude driver on the road beside you.

As we encourage one another to smile and share the joy of the Lord, we also need to encourage one another to cry together as we struggle through the hurts and pains of life. And as we continue to give people permission to cry and smile, the good news is that the Lord is there in the midst of the hurts and

What is another word for "synonym"?

hoorays, enabling us to share our feelings with people around us who can support and comfort us and rejoice with us.

There is certainly much more to our faith than simply smiling all day. But smiles are one way to connect with people and allow them to know that the Lord is certainly alive and well in our hearts and lives. Proverbs 15:13 says it well: "A happy heart makes the face cheerful." And a forgiving Lord allows us to share this joy with others through the gift of smiles!

Thanks, Lord, for that little girl who couldn't smile. I hope she is lighting up the world with her newfound gift! Help us do likewise!

GROWING OLD— GRATEFULLY...

Some of the most lighthearted people I know are of the over-65 variety. They seem to enjoy life, enjoy people, and enjoy the variety of their lifestyles. They remind me of the saying, "You don't stop smiling because you grow older, you grow older because you stop smiling!"

Why are antiques so old?!

Here is a poem that models what it is like to look at old age and enjoy it by being able to laugh at what happens as we age. It was written by an unknown older adult and adapted for our use.

Just a line to say I'm living,
That I'm not among the dead,
Though I'm getting more forgetful,
And something's slipping in my head.

I got used to arthritis,
To my dentures I'm resigned.
I can manage my bifocals,
But, oh, how much I miss my mind.

For sometimes I cannot remember
When I stand atop the stairs,
If I must go down for something
Or if I've just come up from there.

And before the fridge, so often,
My mind is filled with nagging doubt.
Have I just put food away, or
Have I come to take some out?

I called a friend not long ago,
When they answered I just moaned.
I hung up quickly without speaking,
For I'd forgotten who I'd phoned.

And when the darkness falls upon me,
I stand alone and scratch my head.
I don't know if I'm retiring
Or just getting out of bed!

Once I stood in my own bathroom,
Wondering if I'd used the pot.
I flushed it just in case I had
And sat down just in case I'd not.

So now if it's my turn to write you,
There's no need for getting sore.
It may be that I think I've written
And don't need to write no more.

So remember that I love you,
And I wish that you were near,
But I must run, its nearly mail time,
So I wish you blessed cheer.

Now I stand beside the mailbox,
With a face so very red.
Instead of mailing you the letter,
I have opened it instead.

Can egg foo young
ever get old?

15

LAUGHING AT AND DURING MEETINGS

It is always good to remember that one of the books of the Bible is *The Acts of the Apostles*, and not the "Meeting of the Apostles." Sure, meetings are necessary and sometimes even helpful, but we are called to action as we share hope and joy with those around us.

A good friend, Pastor August Mennicke, penned the following during one of his more "exciting" meet-

If something is "needless to say", why is it always said?

ings a few years back. It is a good reminder of how we use words and phrases, as well as what meetings are all about. Thanks for your insights, Augie!

THOUGHTS WHILE DOODLING AND REFLECTING ON A MEETING

In establishing meaningful objectives and priorities with an awareness of the impact of potential and actual relevant variables, the church must consciously reflect on the perceived understanding of its enabling and supportive functions of undergirding and facilitating the congregation's efforts to establish meaningful networking systems that will be compatible with the felt needs of the parish and will inter-face with the most relevant technologies allow-ing for appropriate dialogue to enhance the interactive functions of leadership, thus offering a process by which the vision of the church will be translated into a strategy that will result in a scenario demonstrating the challenges to the church in significantly impacting both the con-ceptual and programmatic development of mod-els reflecting the felt needs of the church, while at the same time establishing appropriate para-meters designed to protect and respect our par-ticular comfort zones and informed by the com-monality of our individual paradigms. This is most certainly true.[3]

HoW Do YoU SPELL C-E-L-E-B-R-A-T-E?

It really was an innocent mistake. There I was, rolling right along as I spelled out the word "celebrate" to emphasize God's love and forgiveness for all of us. The *l* in celebrate, represented "love," and I emphasized Romans 8:38–39, which stresses that nothing will ever separate us from the love of God that is in Christ Jesus our Lord.

Wow, what a message! But I became so enthralled in the message that I moved from the *l* of celebrate to the *b* of celebrate, totally forgetting the letter *e*.

After the message was over, it suddenly hit me. I misspelled celebrate! How in the world had I managed to do that? What a dummy!

Then I thought the best thing to do was to wait to see how the people reacted to me after the service. As the adults, children, and youth left the assembly, a number of them had some nice smiles and kind remarks about the message. I was beginning to feel pretty good again. Then reality struck—a little boy, 7 or 8 years old, came up and looked me straight in the eye, and said, "You misspelled 'celebrate.' You forgot one of the letters!"

Oh, the gifts young children bring to us old and

wise folks! But the irony in all of this was that the letter I forgot, *e*, stood for "everyone." God's love is for everyone, for little kids who point out our faults and for us "big kids" who misspell words like "celebrate"!

It was a real learning experience for me. In my message, I was trying to make the point that it sometimes is easier to accept God's love generally and to realize that He has taken care of the big things in life, such as death and life, angels and demons, present and future, and all of the other powers that try to take God's love away from us. But the struggle I sometimes have is that it is the "little things" in life, the times I goof up, the times I fail to love others, and even the

Does eating Froot Loops or Cheez Whiz affect your spelling ability?!

times I misspell words, that prevent me from seeing the constant and unconditional forgiveness and love of Jesus Christ to each of us.

Thanks, little guy, for pointing out my faults so I can better comprehend God's unconditional love for me, even in the midst of misspellings. Thanks for ministering to me and for helping me experience God's love in a real and honest way. Thanks, child of God, for sharing with me the joys and the realization that it doesn't really matter how we spell c-e-l-e-b-r-a-t-e;

instead the important thing is to know that we are loved and forgiven in the Lord, and by each other.

With Romans 8:38–39, I can boldly say, "I am convinced that neither death nor life, neither angels nor demons, neither present nor future, nor any powers, neither height nor depth, nor anything else"—even misspelling celebrate—"will be able to separate us from the love of God that is in Christ Jesus our Lord"!

Now that's what I call a real celebration, regardless of how I spell it!

Why do children spell farm, "E-I-E-I-O"?

17

LISTENING TO THE SOUNDS OF KIDS

One evening during a violent thunderstorm, a mother was tucking her young son into bed. She was about to turn off the light when he asked with a tremor in his voice, "Mommy, will you sleep with me tonight?"

The mother smiled and gave him a reassuring hug. "I can't, dear," she said. "I have to sleep in Daddy's room."

A long silence was broken at last by his shaking little voice, "The big sissy."

Look and listen around you for other voices of young children. They speak worlds of truths, feelings, and wonderment. They help us older folks better understand what is going on in their little minds, as well as in our little minds!

Joy and wonderment come about when we try to listen "beyond the words" spoken by those around us. We sometimes load so much meaning in our words that we fail to really grasp the message that others are trying to share with us. Especially little kids.

There's another story about a sweet little girl who asks her daddy, "What's sex?" So her father sits her down and tells her all about conception, sperm and eggs, puberty, and many other aspects of sexuality. *After all*, he thinks, *let's tell everything since she has asked.*

The little girl is somewhat awestruck and bewildered. Her father finally asks, "So what made you ask about sex?"

"Oh, Mommy said lunch would be ready in a couple of secs ..."

We listen, we respond, we regroup, we try again, we attempt to hear the great messages of hope and life through the many words flying all around us.

And we live in forgiveness in Christ that allows us to pick up the pieces of our shattered lives and move on again, reassured by His love and care for us.

What do you call it when a horse gets a cramp in one of its legs?

"DOWN UNDER,"
DOWN UNDER

It was a real honor to be invited to speak to the Lutheran Educators' Conference in Melbourne, Australia. The theme would be "The Care and Feeding of the Lutheran Educator." I would share with them ways to keep themselves healthy as they served the Lord and the church. It would be a great chance to mention Wheat Ridge Ministries in the presentation also. A perfect plan.

But the Lord had other plans. As soon as we arrived in the land "down under," I came down with a cantankerous case of shingles. What a great sense of humor God has! Here I was forced to cancel my lectures on "health and healing" because I was sick. *Lord,* I was compelled to pray, *You still are in control of our lives, even though we might think otherwise.*

The good news is that the Aussies showered us with much love and care. My wife, Hazel, got to take her 20 rolls of photos (mostly of kangaroos), and we returned home for further treatment and much reflection. One humorous chap even suggested that during Christmas we now have a new hymn to sing—"Shingle Bells"! Weird humor, right mate? It reminded me of the time a man walked into the doctor's office and was asked, "What do you have?" "Shingles," he replied. The receptionist told him to sit down, remove all of his clothes, and wait in the room for the doctor. The doctor came in, looked him up and down, and asked, "Where? I don't see any."

"Oh, they're out on the truck. Where do you want me to unload them?"

Think of a time when your plans were changed because of illness or some other situation. How did you manage it? Can you look back now and see any humor in it?

Do chickens ever get "people" pox?!

19

i CAN ONLY PLEASE ONE PERSON

*I can only please
one person a day,
and today
ain't your day!*

*(Tomorrow ain't lookin'
too good either.)*

DON'T LET THE KIDS HAVE ALL THE FUN!

Aren't kids great? They are bouncy, fun-loving, trusting, anxious to learn, full of pep and vigor. And believe it or not, many adults are the same way. There seems to be a self-fulfilling prophecy that states that "fun" is primarily for children. Sure, they can be happy-go-lucky; what do they have to worry about? Just wait until they become old enough to have problems and hardships on their own!

The truth is, however, that many children are not fun-loving and full of pep. Many have major problems and struggles already in their early years. And, believe it or not, many adults continue to be fun-loving, even in the midst of their woes and despair.

Have you ever gone to a bookstore and asked where the self-help section is?!

What's the point? We need to affirm that real joy comes from the Lord to both children and adults. Real celebration in life is grounded in faith in Christ Jesus. And that means that all people—young, old, and in-between—have the opportunities to receive the gift of joy and hope.

Maybe kids are a little closer to that "childlike faith" because they are able to trust and believe in things more readily, before being tarnished by experience. Watch for the true joy and energy of many children. It's like the little girl who was asked where her grandmother lived. "Oh, she lives at the airport," she replied. "How can that be?" asked the adult. "Well," she said, "whenever we want her, we just go out there and pick her up."

For us adults, maybe it would be helpful to regain some of that zest for life. Why not try some of these actions in the days ahead. They can give you a lift and certainly will create good discussion with the adult friends around you.

* Give someone a big hug around the neck.
* Blow the wrapper off a straw.
* Ask, "Why?" a lot to your friends.
* Lie on your back and find pictures in the clouds.
* Make a list of everything you want for your next birthday.
* Sit on Santa's lap next Christmas season.
* Eat ice cream for breakfast.
* Take a 5-year-old child to lunch this week.
* Ride a roller coaster.
* Have someone read you a story.
* Sing into your hairbrush.

* Make a milk mustache.
* Step cautiously over sidewalk cracks.
* Refuse to eat crusts.
* Make a face the next time someone says no.

Fun in life is a gift from the Lord, certainly for children, but most certainly for us old folks too. Yes, this is most certainly true!

Don't you wish the mute button on remote controls would work on people?!

21

LETTER FROM CAMP

Summer camp is great fun, but it can also bring different reactions and learnings from both parents and their offspring. One way that humor is used to celebrate life is to look at life and then give it a "tweak." Turn your life experiences around a little. Look at life from another angle, then search for the humor and humanness in all of life.

Here is a sample letter from camp that attempts to do just that.

Dear Mom and Dad,

We are having a great time here at Lake Typhoid. Scoutmaster Webb is making us all write to our parents in case you saw the flood on TV and worried. We are okay. Only one of our tents and two sleeping bags got washed away. Luckily, none of us got drowned because we were all up on the mountain looking for Chad when it happened. Oh yes, please call Chad's mother and tell her he is okay. He can't write because of the cast. We never would have found him in the dark if it hadn't been for the lightning. Scoutmaster Webb got mad at Chad for going on a hike alone without telling anyone. Chad said he did tell him, but it was dur-

ing the fire so he probably didn't hear him. Did you know that if you put gas on a fire, the gas can will blow up? The wet wood still didn't burn, but one of our tents did. Also some of our clothes. John is going to look weird until his hair grows back. We will be home on Saturday if Scoutmaster Webb gets the car fixed. It wasn't his fault about the wreck. The brakes worked okay when we left. Scoutmaster Webb said that with a car that old, you have to expect something to break down; that's probably why he can't get insurance on it. We think it's a neat car. He doesn't care if we get it dirty, and if it's hot, sometimes he lets us ride on the tailgate. It gets pretty hot with ten people in a car. He let us take turns riding in the trailer until the highway patrolman stopped and talked to us. Scoutmaster Webb is a neat guy. Don't worry, he is a good driver.

He is teaching Terry how to drive. But he only lets him drive on the mountain roads where there isn't any traffic. All we ever see up there are logging trucks. This morning all of the guys were diving off the rocks and swimming out in the lake. Scoutmaster Webb wouldn't let me because I can't swim and Chad was afraid he would sink because of his cast, so he let us take the canoe across the lake. It was great. You can still see some of the trees under the water from the flood. Scoutmaster Webb isn't crabby like some scoutmasters. He didn't even get mad about the life jackets. He has to spend a lot of time working on the car so we are trying not to cause him any trouble. Guess what? We have all passed our first-aid merit badges. When Dave dove in the lake and cut his arm, we got to see how a tourniquet works. Also Wade and I threw up. Scoutmaster Webb said it probably was just food poisoning from the leftover chicken. I have to go now. We are going into town to mail our letters and buy bullets. Don't worry about anything. We are fine.

Love,

Ralphie

P.S. How long has it been since I had a tetanus shot?

If a young dog wanted to go camping, would it use a pup tent?

22

TO PLAY AND
TO PRAY

As God's healthy and hope-filled people, we are called to play and to pray. Too often, we take ourselves too seriously. We need to "lighten up" and enjoy the gifts that our Lord continues to give to us. We need to play, to enjoy, to laugh because we know that the victory is already won for us—by Christ!

Why is it that churches and church people seem so serious and mournful, while at the same time the Lord of Scripture is so mirthful and full of life? Something has gone wrong with our interpretation of Scripture!

We also need to pray more intentionally. And as we pray, we need to be ready for God to answer our prayers—in His way.

If you are like I am, some of my prayers are still selfish and one-sided. Like some of these prayers heard recently:

* "Lord, help me to relax about insignificant details, beginning tomorrow at 7:41 A.M. EST."

* "God, help me to try not to run everything. But if You need some help, feel free to ask me."

* "God, help me to do only what I can and trust

You for the rest. And would You mind putting that in writing?"

✳ "Lord, keep me open to others' ideas, wrong though they may be!"

To play and to pray—two basic elements for a person with a joy-filled faith. Prayer helps us to stay connected to the Lord, and play helps us to celebrate with those around us.

To show another example of the efficacy of prayers, there is the story of a church that was growing very quickly in a small town—until an adult night club opened right next door to it. The church leaders were shocked. They had to get rid of it. So they prayed to the Lord to strike that building down—through lightning, floods, or whatever.

Two weeks later, sure enough, lightning struck the club and burned it to the ground. The manager of the night club took the church to court and tried to prove that they were guilty. The church leaders pleaded with the judge that it was not their fault. They didn't do anything wrong!

After much discussion, the wise judge settled the two sides down and quietly observed: "How very interesting. Here we have a case of a night club owner who believes in prayer—and a church who doesn't!"

Pray and play—praise the Lord!

Have you ever wanted to order some eggs and some chicken at a restaurant to see which comes first?!

23

I'VE GOT THE JOY, JOY, JOY...

Remember that old familiar camp song, "I've got the joy, joy, joy, joy down in my heart ..."? What a good way to remind us of the love of the Lord that brings this joy, joy, joy to us each day.

It is amazing how recent studies point to the fact that joy and delight in life actually bring positive effects to one's heart and health. Proverbs 15:30 is right on target in terms of the effects of joy on our bodies: "A cheerful look brings joy to the heart, and good news gives health to the bones." Also check out Proverbs 15:13: "A happy heart makes the face cheerful, but heartache crushes the spirit."

The late Henri Nouwen wrote often about joy and sadness in life. He told the story about a friend of his who radiated joy in his life, not because his life was easy, but because he habitually recognized God's presence in the midst of human suffering—his own as well as others. He said that his friend's joy was contagious. The more he was with his friend, the more he caught glimpses of the sun shining through the clouds. "Yes, I know there is a sun," Nouwen stated, "even though the skies are covered with clouds." But it was the sun that allowed him to see the clouds! Nouwen closed his remarks by stating, "Those who keep speaking about the sun while walking under a cloudy sky are messengers of hope, the true saints of our day!"[4]

Yes, we've got the joy, joy, joy of the Lord—and we're glad!

What was the best thing before sliced bread?!

24

TOP 10 LIST
OF HOW TO KEEP
HAPPY AND HEALTHY
AS A FAMILY OF GOD!

(WITH APOLOGIES TO DAVID LETTERMAN)

"When there are children in our life, it's always dancing season—even if we must occasionally dance with a limp!"[5] What a good summary of the frustrations and joys that come to families as we continue to celebrate life in the Lord.

Here is a "Top 10" list from one such family who takes very seriously the need to keep a strong sense of humor in our daily lives as moms, dads, kids, and grandparents. As someone once said, "A keen sense of humor helps us to overlook the unbecoming, understand the unconventional, tolerate the unpleasant, overcome the unexpected, and outlast the unbearable."

10 "He who laughs, lasts!" Our family has taken seriously these words of Martin Luther, or whoever said it. Being able to laugh with each other and not at each other is a gift families can develop. Take time to learn to laugh at yourself, then laugh with each other. The gift of laughter is a visible sign of the forgiveness in Christ Jesus.

9 Develop family traditions that become meaningful opportunities for family relationships and sharing. It is encouraging for parents to see their children developing traditions in their own lives as they begin to build families. Special trips during holidays, decorating the Christmas tree as a family, birthday celebrations, making an Advent wreath together, coloring Easter eggs, going sledding, have all become traditions in our family that keep us connected and close to one another. If your family has not been able to develop some meaningful traditions, why not start now with some small activity that you can replicate regularly throughout the years ahead?

8 If parents argue in front of their children, they also need to forgive in front of their children. In our early years as a family, we realized we would have disagreements while the kids were present (and many times these disagreements centered around one or more of the kids!). However, we also realized that when we would forgive each other, the kids were long gone in bed or doing something else. It has been helpful to us to develop the covenant that when arguments do occur, forgiveness also needs to happen with the same parties involved. It sure makes forgiveness more real, and our "constructive conflicts" are seen as ways to share forgiveness.

7 Play games together. Whether as a couple or an entire family, board games, card games, and recreational games can keep us all happy and healthy. In our "older years," Hazel and I have enjoyed some of these party games for older adults: "Musical Recliners," "Shufflescotch," "Red Rover, Red Rover, Send Antacids on Over," "Spin the Hot Water Bottle," and our all-time favorite, "Hide and Go Soak."

6 Forget about hearing some of the "things you'd love to hear" from your kids. We all have wish lists of phrases we'd like to hear from our offspring, but don't hold your breath until you hear the following:

* "Sure, Dad, I'll pick up the check."
* "Pass the broccoli, please."
* "No thanks, it's too expensive."
* "Bored? How could I be bored?"
* "I've already made my bed."
* "It was my fault."
* "That's okay. None of my friends are allowed to do it either."
* "Who cares if the TV is broken?"

5 As a family, be inverse paranoids. That is, convince each other that everyone in your family is out to make everyone else happy. Accuse peo-

ple in your family of trying to make one another happy—it works!

4 Spend time together. This one can really be a "guilt trip," but it needs to be said. Quality time is good, but quantity time is also needed. Work hard at trying to "do nothing" together as a family.

3 Keep happy and healthy as a family by asking other families how they keep happy and healthy. No family is an island; we are all connected to each other by the waters of Baptism.

2 Say nice things to each other—regularly. Give "I was caught doing something right" awards to your kids. Leave love notes on the refrigerator when you leave in the morning. Drop a postcard to your grandson to let him know you're thinking of him today. Share your love, and God's love too, with each of your family members in personal ways.

1 Laugh out loud with each other! Laughter is the jam on the toast of life. It adds flavor, keeps it from being too dry, and makes it easier to swallow. We can laugh because we know how it all turns out in the end—Christ is victorious!

Shouldn't married couples stay away from water beds so they don't drift apart?

We are kept happy and healthy as families of God because of our Lord Jesus Christ. Laughter is God's hand on the shoulder of a troubled world and troubled families. Holy laughter is a gift of grace. It is the human spirit's last defense against sin and despair. Laughter is a blunt, brilliant, brave affirmation that death is not the final answer. Holy mirth is keeping sight of Christ's final victory over death.

John 15:11 says it so well: "I have told you this so that My joy may be in you and that your joy may be complete."

How about making your own "Top 10" list of ways to help your family and others keep happy and healthy as a family of God? And rejoice in the Lord as we celebrate with our families, knowing that through the pain and frustration and despair of daily life, the joy of the Lord continues to be our source of comfort, hope, and, yes, even laughter!

Before television, did people eat frozen radio dinners?

i AM SPECiAL!
(i REALLY AM!)

Rachel's teacher saw her in the church hall last Sunday and said, "Rachel, you sure look pretty today!"

"I know I am!" the 4-year-old giggled. She knows she is a special person of God.

Rachel's teacher was affirming in this little child of God that she is somebody special. And Rachel was eager to accept this sense of love and belonging. Was she boasting about it? Not really, but she sure was bubbly about it.

Is it possible to be totally partial?

I continue to thank God and marvel at the wonderful ways teachers, parents, and grandparents continue to show and tell others they are special in God's eyes. And we do this by letting those around us know they are special in our eyes as well. The world continues to overload us with shame and guilt in so many ways. And how great it is to hear the affirming words of a teacher, of a friend, of a parent, cutting through that shame and guilt and helping kids of all ages to remember whose they are.

Jack Kemp, political figure and former quarterback for the Buffalo Bills, tells how his college football coach called him in one day and confided in him that each year there was one player he kept his eye on because he saw in this player a special quality. Kemp was told that this year he was the one player who had great potential to develop into a real winner. The coach then told Mr. Kemp that he should keep this conversation to himself and no one, especially no one on the team, was to know because anyone with whom he discussed it would become very upset.

Kemp reports that after he left the locker room that day, he was ready to run through a brick wall for the coach. And he did—all year long. Kemp continues the story by saying he found out later the coach had virtually the same chat with every other guy on the squad. It was a tremendous way to encourage and affirm his players.

There are too many kids in this world who are growing up with the "TNT" philosophy of life—meaning "There's No Tomorrow." Our role as people of God is to continue to show others that Jesus Christ is the hope of the world, as well as the hope for each of us individually. We continue to see and hear people who feel alienated from God, from themselves, and from others. They live with a deep sense of worthlessness. "I am not good enough. I never will be good enough. I

Can you be a closet claustrophobic?!

am not lovable." These people have a hard time distinguishing between "I made a mistake" and "I am a mistake." We all continue to make mistakes, and God continues to forgive us and move us on. But He never sees *us* as a mistake. Instead, He sees us as His children, created, redeemed, and loved as worthwhile people.

My prayer is that I can learn from Rachel, whom God continues to love, so I can hear myself and others say and sense that "I am special, I really am." And all because of our special God—and He really is too!

26

DO BE DO BE DO!

That old crooner, Frank Sinatra, really knew what he was talking about. Quite theological too! I would like to suggest that "Do Be Do Be Do" is an excellent ministry theme for God's people. Whether we are in the workplace, school, home, church, or neighborhood, "Do Be Do Be Do" says it all.

It is our theme song—the Lord has called us to be "Do Be Do Be Do" people.

Hear it in other words from the Scriptures:

* "You are a chosen people, a royal priesthood, a holy nation, people belonging to God ..." (1 Peter 2:9).

* "You are the people of God; He loved you and chose you for His own" (Colossians 3:12 TEV).

Throughout Scripture, God affirms that we are His people. Our role is to be those people because He loves us and continues to forgive us and give us strength in the Spirit. One large part of our "Do Be Do Be Do" ministry style is to BE the people of God that we are.

More words from the Lord:

* "I will show you my faith by what I do" (James 2:18).

✱ "And what does the LORD require of you? To act justly and to love mercy and to walk humbly with your God" (Micah 6:8).

In addition to being God's people, we also are doers of the Word. And as we go about our daily life in the Lord, we join friend Frank in chanting our liturgy of doing and being the people of God.

Why not post this "mission statement" on your refrigerator? Or put it on your wall or even in your car. And on days when you or I feel we haven't done enough for the Lord, listen for the Spirit to remind us that we are first of all people of God, and because of that, we are able to do great things for Him, even on days when we fail. Or on days when we get so wrapped up in the doing of all our ministry, listen for the Spirit to remind us once again that we are not

What is "ado," and why shouldn't there be any more of it?!

just doers but first of all, we are the people of God because of our Baptism in Christ Jesus.

Not a bad statement with which to live each day. And not a bad statement to remind us of who we are and to allow us to shout our "Do Be Do Be Do" song to those the Lord will put into our lives and hearts in the coming days and weeks.

As "Do Be Doers," we can joyfully proclaim with St. Paul that "everything you do or say then, should be done in the name of the Lord Jesus, as you give thanks through Him to God the Father" (Colossians 3:17 TEV).

Thanks, Mr. Sinatra, for the plug. Thanks for getting us moving in the right direction. But above all, thanks, Lord, for coming to us in wonderfully miraculous ways to move us once again to exciting days ahead.

Do Be Do Be Do—look out world, here we come!

When sheep can't sleep, do they count people?

27

THEOLOGY OF T-SHIRTS

It used to be billboards, then refrigerator magnets. But now to understand the various philosophies of contemporary life, we need only read the T-shirts that pass us by in the malls, in schools, and even in our own homes. Let's look at a few of these walking pieces of theology that have passed my way recently.

* Life isn't over until the fat man eats your cookies!
* I'm not aging—I'm marinating.
* Baseball is life—the rest is just details.
* Life is hard—then you die.
* Hug a firefighter—feel warm all over.
* Listen, honey, nobody knows how to raise teenagers. You just live through it, and one day they're people.
* Young at heart—slightly older in other places.
* If you don't like my attitude, call 1-800-WHO-CARES.
* I may not be rich and famous, but my grand-children are priceless.
* In the beginning was the word, and the word was chocolate, and it was good (Confections 1.5 ounces, 240 calories).
* I'm busy, you're boring—have a nice day.
* Make the ball lie in green pastures, not in still

waters (Arnie 3, par 72).

* Places to go, people to annoy.
* I'm so impatient I'm looking for a crash course on patience.
* How many Lutherans does it take to change a lightbulb? Change? Why change?

Did Dr. Freud's wife wear Freudian slips?

What does all this mean? (Not a bad slogan for a Lutheran T-shirt, by the way!) It means that obviously we are living around and in the midst of different philosophies of life. It means that now more than ever we need to intentionally verbalize and demonstrate our faith in the Lord Jesus Christ in strong, firm, and celebrative ways.

It means that in the midst of pain and frustration, it's important to lighten up. It means that we need to listen to people and to the messages on their T-shirts. It means that people do not just read our T-shirts, they "read" our lives in terms of how we respond, listen, and react to them and their needs.

How do people read our appearance, our habits, our words? What message are we giving out? Perhaps more than wearing T-shirts that joyfully tell the message of health and hope in the name of the Lord Jesus, we need to wear a shirt that simply says, "Loved by God—and I'm glad!"

TO CELEBRATE LIFE MEANS TO SHARE LIFE

It is one thing to celebrate life and enjoy all of our gifts; it's quite another thing to celebrate life while sharing these gifts with others. Happiness, for example, is not something we do, but something we experience by sharing our gifts and lives with other people. Joy in the Lord comes to people who celebrate life by giving their life away to others. We are gifted to be servants of the Lord. We have been blessed to be blessings to others. And to whom much has been given—yes, you guessed it, much is expected!

This wonderful and touching "Cookie Thief" story helps support the fact that our role is to receive, thank the Lord, and share the blessings we have received. Thank you to the anonymous author for this significant story.

THE COOKIE THIEF

A woman was waiting at an airport one night
With several long hours before her flight.
She hunted for a book in the airport shop,
Bought a bag of cookies, and found a place to drop.

She was engrossed in her book but happened to see
That the man beside her, as bold as could be,
Grabbed a cookie or two from the bag between,
Which she tried to ignore, to avoid a scene.

She read, munched cookies, and watched the clock
As the gutsy "cookie thief" diminished her stock.
She was getting more irritated as the minutes ticked by,
Thinking, "If I wasn't so nice, I'd blacken his eye!"

With each cookie she took, he took one too.
When only one was left, she wondered what he'd do.
With a smile on his face and a nervous laugh,
He took the last cookie and broke it in half.

He offered her half as he ate the other.
She snatched it from him and thought, "Oh brother,
This guy has some nerve, and he's also rude,
Why, he didn't even show any gratitude!"

She had never known when she had been so galled
And sighed with relief when her flight was called.
She gathered her belongings and headed for the gate,
Refusing to look back at the "thieving ingrate."

She boarded the plane and sank in her seat,
Then sought her book, which was almost complete.
As she reached in her baggage, she gasped with surprise.
There was her bag of cookies in front of her eyes!

"If mine are here," she moaned with despair,
"Then the others were his, and he tried to share!"
Too late to apologize, she realized with grief,
That she was the rude one, the ingrate, the thief!

Author unknown

76

29

CHAIN LAUGHTER

A necessary ingredient in having a positive sense of humor is being able to laugh at ourselves. Here is a "chain letter" that has been used for years and continues to bring joy and laughter (I hope!) to pastors and other church workers. It is to the credit of our professional church workers that they are able to chuckle at this story and laugh, at least most of the time, at themselves. I strongly believe that whoever is not able to laugh at himself or herself and has become so serious in life, has also given up on the Lord.

You be the judge of this little story.

Try this chain letter. It is meant to bring relief and happiness to you. Unlike other chain letters, it does not cost money. Simply send a copy of this letter to six other churches who are tired of their pastors. Then bundle up your pastor and send him to the church at the top of the list.

Add your name to the bottom of the list. In one week, you will receive 16,436 pastors, and one should be a dandy.

Have faith in this letter. One church broke the chain and got their old pastor back!

Thanks, pastors and other church workers, for the ability to laugh at yourselves. And keep laughing. It's only just begun!

THE GOOD FRIDAYS AND EASTERS OF OUR LIVES

Hoorays and hurts … life and death … ups and downs … light and darkness … Law and Gospel … Good Friday and Easter …

Life is indeed a paradox. We continue to live—and celebrate—smack dab in the middle of all the "ifs" and "buts" and "in spite ofs" and "nevertheless" and "therefores" of life. The reason for this is the most important paradox of all: We celebrate Easter as today not because we have forgotten Good Friday, but because we remember Good Friday.

A friend of mine always begins a novel by reading the last chapter first. That's no fair! You spoil the whole sequence and flow.

Wrong, he states emphatically. By reading the last chapter first, he claims that he can better appreciate and better concentrate on the rest of the story, spending more time on the major plot and characters, because he knows how it turns out.

How true of our lives also. The importance of the endings—the resurrection experiences—are only marvelous in conjunction with the crucifixion and death experiences that we have to go through first. But it's knowing the ending that makes it possible to go through the "rest of the story" at all—and to celebrate in the process. We know how Christ's passion story ends—He is alive! Therefore we can celebrate that first He was willing to die. And we know how our story will end—we will be alive with Him in heaven! Therefore we can also celebrate through the Good Fridays of our lives, leaving time and energy to concentrate on smaller details, such as loving and forgiving and caring for others and celebrating our faith together.

Take time to read that last chapter again. And remember it through all the other chapters so every page of your life can be part of a "Happy Good Friday—Happy Easter!" kind of story.

If big elephants have big trunks, do small elephants have suitcases?

LiFE iS FOR-GiViNG!

Life is for-giving and forgiving is for life!

The key to family relationships is the forgiveness we have in Jesus Christ. It allows us to start and end each day fresh in the Gospel message of Christ's forgiveness of us. It keeps us fresh, focused, and fulfilled as people in God's community.

I like the business card of a friend of mine, which simply states, "Forgiveness Is My Business!" If one thing separates people of God from the values and behaviors of society, it is how we treat and relate to one another. And even when I do not model or act out my faith as a forgiven person of God, I know that I am still forgiven and able to move on to the next day. That's the joy of forgiveness: Even when we're not forgivable, the Lord forgives!

Have you ever heard any of these sayings around your household?

* "I forgive you, but don't let it happen again!"
* "Just forgive and forget."
* "I'll forgive you, but I'll never forget."
* "I can never forgive you for that!"

And even in the midst of these harsh statements, we regularly hear our Lord saying to each of us, "I forgive you all your sins, in the name of the Father, and of the Son, and of the Holy Spirit. Amen."

As we live out a life of forgiveness in our families, we continue to remind each other that forgiveness is not a word, a concept, or just a doctrine. Instead, "forgiveness" is a person, Jesus Christ. A family prayer book years ago said it this way:

Has anyone actually bought a sidewalk or garage at a sale?

FORGIVENESS IS A PERSON

We've been fooled long enough, Lord. Forgiveness isn't a word that should be used only on Sunday mornings.

No, forgiveness is a person—a person who loves You and shares love with me and others around him.

Let's get the word "forgiveness" out of the catechism and hymnbook and dictionary and into the lives and hands and voices of people, where it belongs.

Forgiveness is a person—starting with You, Lord![6]

I was struck recently by reading the story of Pastor Walter Everett, who officiated at the wedding of a young couple, Sandie and Mike. There was nothing unusual about this wedding, except that seven and a half years earlier, the groom had shot and killed Pastor Everett's 24-year-old son.

Pastor Everett states: "Many have asked me how I could forgive something as big as the death of my son and how I could forget what had happened. But to say this is to imply that forgiving is forgetting. It is not. As a friend of mine has reminded me, 'Forgiving is remembering and moving on.' For me to forgive was to make a conscious decision, with the help of God, to refuse to let anger control me any longer. When God enabled me to let go of that anger, I became free to forgive him."

Have you ever stared at a can of orange juice because it says, "concentrate"?

WE GIVE FORGIVENESS

You've heard the story of the married couple who agreed to never go to bed angry and that one of them would take a walk on nights when there were disagreements and arguments. On their 50th wedding anniversary, the husband credited their agreement as being very helpful in keeping them together for half a century. And he also felt that all of his long walks in the fresh air in the evening also had been good for his health.

What is forgiveness—really? A young girl said it well. When asked to give a definition of forgiveness, she said, "It is the odor that flowers breathe when they are trampled on." Somehow, forgiveness looks beyond what one does. It helps you and me to look at people and their actions and reactions through the cross and the empty tomb. It helps us keep life in perspective. Forgiveness is not the ability to forget the hurts in your relationship with a spouse, child, or neighbor. It is the process of remembering our Lord and His forgiveness of us, then moving on.

What does all this mean in our day-to-day relationships in the home? For me, it means that we need to help each other focus on the Lord and what He has already done for us—forgiven us! It means that sometimes we just need to take walks after arguments so in the fresh air we might find the freshness of forgiveness. It means that I do not try to coerce and control someone else's behavior by threatening to forgive or not to forgive. It means that I need to work hard at sharing forgiveness with those who wronged me the same way the Lord shares forgiveness with me as I continue to wrong Him. It means that the statement, "I forgive you, but don't let it happen again," should never be uttered where two or more people are gathered. And it also means that even when it is uttered, the Lord forgives us and allows us to move on to another day of fresh forgiveness in Him.

WE CAN'T GO BACK

Too often families are stymied because we get caught up in trying to relive the past. We try to make it better. We try to erase the hurts. We try to "forgive and forget." When you and I are filled with grief and regret over our past mistakes, we need to remember that we cannot go back and make a new beginning, but we can start today and make a new ending.

Forgiveness is our business. It's the business of families. It's the business of the family of God. Life really is for-giving!

THOUGHTS TO CONSIDER AND SHARE:

1 When is it hardest for you to forgive someone?

2 When is it easiest?

3 Think of people in your life who are "good" at forgiving. What makes them so effective?

4 Who in your family needs some words of forgiveness right now? (Well, what are you waiting for?)

5 Do you have any past regrets and mistakes that continue to haunt you? With whom can you share your hurts? Allow the Spirit to help you make a new ending. Give it a try.

LAUGHTER—
AN ENCOURAGING
SIGN OF THE
PRESENCE OF GOD

God gave humans the ability to laugh. While animals enjoy themselves, we do not see them sitting around laughing and telling stories. It's their loss.

Laughter is a gift based on the joy we have in Christ Jesus. It is grounded in the gift of faith won for us by Christ's death and resurrection. It breaks tension, lifts spirits, sets people at ease, builds bridges, creates positive mind-sets toward life, and

Why do 7-Eleven stores have locks on their doors when they are open 24 hours?

85

keeps people healthier by releasing endorphins throughout the body.

Laughter is a sign of God's blessings. In the Old Testament, countless stories are told of the joy of God's people. Verses such as Psalm 126:2, "Our mouths are filled with laughter, our tongues with songs of joy," are echoed over and over throughout Scripture.

Laughter is a sign that we are enjoying God's blessings. As a brother I saw recently states, "He who no longer knows how to laugh, or smile, is only waiting to die."

Laughter is not the absence of tears. In fact, they usually go together in human experiences. In Christ, the joy is knowing that laughter follows tears because Good Friday is followed by Easter!

Rejoice, laugh, celebrate—for God is with us!

Would a neurotic owl say "Why? Why?"

WHERE HAS ALL THE LAUGHTER GONE?

Can you imagine a world without laughter? The absence of laughter may be a dangerous sign of the absence of God. It would certainly be a world without children.

In *The Screwtape Letters*, C. S. Lewis portrays the enemy of joy and laughter as the devil himself. Screwtape (the devil) doesn't really understand the laughter that is a result of joy—he only knows it bothers him. "We do not know the real cause of laughter," he writes. "… laughter of this kind does us no good and should always be discouraged." Screwtape goes on to say that laughter and its results "promotes charity, courage, contentment, and many other evils."[7]

When we find ourselves in very serious company where there is absolutely no place for a sense of humor, it is a spiritual warning sign. Have you been in any such places recently? What was going on there? How did you respond? What else could have been done to bring joy and hope?

We live in a world that is "joy impaired." We are surrounded by "chronic seriousness." You and I are called to bring sights and sounds of hope and joy to this world, motivated by the joy and hope given to us by the Holy Spirit. Joy to the world, the Lord has come—through us!

Is there anyone with
a wet sense of humor?

THiNGS TO DO
FoR FUN AT HoME

Our family has enjoyed life together through many ups and downs by working hard at keeping a sense of humor through all of life's travails. By taking the Lord very seriously at His Word, and ourselves not too seriously, we have managed to cry and laugh and support each other for more than 38 years—in a row!

Here are a number of things we've done through the years to keep us, and our friends, on our toes.

Phone Answering Machines. Most people have them, and that's good. But so many of them are so-o-o boring, right? So our family tries to lighten ours up with messages such as these:

"Hi, you've reached Rich and Hazel's home. We're out counting our blessings right now, and you no doubt are one of them—that is, unless you are trying to sell us something ..."

Or, *"Hi, you've reached Rich and Hazel's car phone. We're home right now, but leave your name and number, and we'll call you when we go out ..."* (My mom never did understand this one—she always wondered how we could afford a car phone!) By the way, we did get rid of our car phone. It was so inconvenient running into the garage to answer it all the time!

2 **Annual Christmas Letters.** This is our favorite family pastime. We still write a composite letter after all these years. Every person has to "sign off," approving all of the letter, before it is sent. The Bimler tradition started when we kept getting all these 18-page, single-spaced Christmas letters from our family and friends that told more than we ever wanted to know about anyone (sorry, relatives). We also observed that all of the children of our friends were getting As in school, playing varsity football, had three part-time jobs, and full rides to exquisite colleges. We looked at our kids and said, "What happened?"

So we started to create an annual Christmas epistle that told funny (we hope) anecdotes about the year past. Here are some samples.

"Rich just finished a new book that reviewers say, 'It's the kind of book that once you put it down, you can't pick it up again!'"

"Hazel continues to take photos of grandkids and bears because she always looks for 'Kodiak' moments."

"The Grandkids—we buy their toys at 'Toys or Else!'"

"Bob—being single, he is always looking for a friend. A young woman approached him in a store the other day and asked, 'Are you unattached?' and Bob said, 'No, I'm just put together loosely!'"

We even were bold enough one year to suggest that, at Christmastime, it is helpful for God's people to bring "gold, frankincense, and mirth" to each other.

See also the complete letter from a recent Christmas, which is located on page 139.

Isn't every place within walking distance, if you have the time?

3 **Photographs.** If photos bring joy, our household is one of the most joyful on record. The only time we do not take pictures is when the "spirit is willing, but the flash is weak."

One of our more daring feats was the time we took a special photo of our first grandchild, Matthew. We, like many others, had looked at thousands of pictures of other grandkids through the years. Sure, they were cute, in a way, but they all looked alike. So to put a little twist on things, we propped little Matthew up in a chair and tried to keep him from flopping over. We then put one of those big noses and glasses on him and—*flash!*—we had a special picture. I carried this photo around with me for months. It was especially fun to watch the eyes of all the folks who looked at the photo. They looked at it, looked away, then did another quick "take." I sometimes would proudly say, "He looks just like his grandmother!"

4 **Sports and games.** Our family continues to enjoy competitive opportunities, though the older we get the less competitive it becomes—probably because I have a hard time beating anyone in anything anymore!

Family times can be fun times. Do what works best for you. And continue to look for ways to share your faith and joy in the Lord through these good times together!

If you jogged backwards,
would you gain weight?

LAUGH,
EVEN THOUGH iT HURTS

The joy of the Christian life is that we can laugh and cry, almost at the same time. So much of life lets us down. So many of our failures and problems continue to haunt us.

For example, isn't it amazing how often we fail to communicate what we want to communicate? Why can't we explain ourselves better? Why do people misunderstand us? Why don't I think more before I talk?

Check out this dialogue and see if you can connect with it.

> A farmer walked into an attorney's office to file for a divorce.
> The attorney asked, "May I help you?"
> The farmer said, "Yeah, I want to get one of them dayvorces."
> The attorney said, "Well, do you have any grounds?"
> The farmer said, "Yeah, I got about 140 acres."
> The attorney said, "No, you don't understand; do you have a case?"
> The farmer said, "No, I don't have a Case, but I have a John Deere."

The attorney said, "No, you don't understand; I mean do you have a grudge?"

The farmer said, "Yeah, I got a grudge, that's where I park my John Deere."

The attorney said, "No, sir, I mean do you have a suit?"

The farmer said, "Yes, sir, I got a suit. I wear it to church on Sundays."

The exasperated attorney said, "Well, sir, does your wife beat you up or anything?"

The farmer said, "No, sir, we both get up about 4:30."

Finally, the attorney said, "Okay, let me put it this way: Why do you want a divorce?"

The farmer replied, "Well, I can never have a meaningful conversation with her."

 What does A.C.R.O.N.Y.M. stand for?

Sound familiar? Even if it is "the story of your life," there is still much room for rejoicing because the Lord is still in charge. Communication from Him is clear: He loves us and forgives us. Communication in Him, through the Holy Spirit, can also be clear. With His help, understanding, and forgiveness, we can reach out to those we try to communicate with, who misunderstand us and whom we misunderstand, and whom we have spoken to in harsh, quick language. Christ's words, unlike ours, bring healing and love into the midst of miscommunication, helping us to laugh, despite the hurt, at what a mess we've made. Now that's meaningful conversation!

HUMOROUS FAMILY VACATIONS OR iT DiDN'T SEEM FUNNY AT THE TiME!

Laughter is a gift from God. Isn't it great that we can use this gift as we remember the "fun times" from our various family vacations? Time is also a gift, and time enables us to form a different perspective on family experiences as we press our "rewind" button and recall some of those hilarious happenings.

Here is a brief peek at snippets from the Bimlers' family vacation album. See if you can find the hidden humor, which was not necessarily evident at the time!

We took two of our grandchildren to Disney World. The problem was we also took their parents. The six of us stayed in one hotel room. You guessed it—Grandpa was paying the bill!

The kids wanted to spend all day in the hotel swimming pool instead of at Disney World. Matt said that every time he saw Mickey Mouse, he got "Disneyspells"!

2 On one excursion to Chicago many years ago, we stopped with our three kids at a restaurant. I was a little "hyper" and wanted to eat quickly and get back on the road. As I was warning Bob and Mike not to spill their milk, I knocked my iced tea glass off the table and onto my lap. The whole family roared, except me!

3 During a car trip through Great Britain, Hazel and I drove along and came to a "roundabout" in the road, where you zip on and circle around until you exit on your desired route. Unfortunately, every time we got on the silly roundabouts, we couldn't figure out how to get off them! Two weeks of going in circles on a roundabout is certainly not a fun vacation.

4 My children's father couldn't find his car keys after returning from a hike in the Colorado mountains. "Oh, look, Dad, there they are on the front seat," said Diane securely. Then she added, "And I locked the car so no one would take the keys!" Needless to say, she and her Dad don't travel together anymore, at least not in the same vehicle.

5 One of Hazel's favorite stories is of the time we were driving through the Grand Tetons. We were happy to be able to experience these majestic mountains as a family. We looked in the back seat and found all three of our offspring asleep. "Wake up, wake up, you'll miss these mountains," we shouted. "That's okay," came a sleepy voice. "We'll just look at the photos Mom takes of them!" Talk about a mountaintop experience!

6 Our three kids were great travelers, except when they were together—in the car, motel, restaurant, pool, or wherever. I still remember getting so upset one time that I pulled the car over and demanded, "Okay, no more arguing and this is the last time I'm going to tell you this!" I felt well satisfied, until Mike's small voice came back, "I'm glad, Dad, because we're tired of hearing that from you!" Needless to say, we left Mike home from all family trips after that!

Can you use travelers' checks in your home town?

Yes, family vacations can be fun, can't they? They allow families to be together, to listen and to share, to laugh and to cry. We wouldn't have it any other way.

To put these vivid ventures into perspective, I remember driving through a heavy and scary snow-storm in Minnesota one winter. Sliding cars every-where, wind chill at 40 below zero, strong north winds hampering visibility. I was nervous, worried, and stressed to the hilt. Just then, something touched my shoulders—a gift from the Lord! It was two hands massaging my neck. It was soothing and felt so good. It was a sign of love and concern. It was a miracle!

It was Bob, my son, massaging my neck. And his words said it so well, "It's okay, Dad, we're going to make it!"

Yes, it was a miracle from God, in the shape of a son, speaking on behalf of his whole family.

Yes, family vacations can be fun—through laughter, time, and the touch of the Lord through family members. But there is one more gift to celebrate—forgiveness, which keeps us focused on the Lord through all of life's journeys.

Enjoy family times as you laugh, remember, forgive, and thank God for each other. Thanks, family, for the memories—now please go back to sleep so we can get an early start in the morning!

May God bless you on your travels!

Do Danish people
have American rolls
for breakfast?

HO-HO-HOME iS WHERE THE HAR-HAR-HEART iS!

Love may make the world go round, but humor and laughter are key ingredients to strengthen and affirm that love throughout each family.

Families are great places to practice daily the joy and necessity of laughter. Parents, children, and grandparents need to take seriously the development of a sense of humor in the home. We need to help "give permission" for people to laugh at themselves in the safe confines of the kitchen and family room, not to mention other places in the house.

A key ingredient in sharing joy and laughter is that it is really not something we do, but something we are. We live out a positive attitude toward life because of the joy and forgiveness that we know our Lord has for us in Jesus Christ. As people who live on this side of the resurrection, we know how things turn out in the end, and therefore, we can boldly laugh and enjoy each other through the daily activities in our home.

A major factor in keeping humor alive in the home is that it is not a matter of how many jokes we tell or how often we do little pranks on each other (though these are both ways to keep a positive attitude going!), but it is the ongoing, day-to-day activities in our families that encourage, affirm, and teach the joy and power of laughter. Robert Coles, in his book *The Moral Intelligence of Children* emphasizes the importance of the "uneventful events" in our daily lives. He says that, in the long run, the everyday moments in day-to-day life turn out to be the most influential.[8] Perhaps it is really true what my mom always said to me—"Little things do mean a lot!" (Although she usually said this when it was time for my allowance.)

The strong words in Deuteronomy 11:18–20a emphasize this principle in very intentional ways as well: "Fix these words of Mine in your hearts and minds; tie them as symbols on your hands and bind them on your foreheads, teach them to your children, talking about them when you sit at home and when

What would happen if you put a humidifier and a dehumidifier in the same room?

you walk along the road, when you lie down and when you get up. Write them on the door frames of your houses and on your gates."

God simply asks us to live our lives as Easter people, through the power of His Spirit. No big sermons. No big preparation for hour-long family devotions. No need to bring a guest theologian into your home for a weekly lecture. Not because these activities wouldn't be helpful, but because the Lord is simply asking us to "talk and walk" a life of faith, of joy, and of forgiveness.

So what does all this mean? First, it means that there is no need to run out and buy the latest joke book. Sharing joy and laughter in the Lord does not mean knowing the favorite "top 10" list or memorizing Jay Leno's monologue. Instead, it means being aware of the presence of the Lord in our families and sharing this joy through common, everyday events. It means laughing together, crying together, and helping all family members see the joy and humor in their daily lives. When our Rice Krispies just lie in our cereal bowl in the morning, without even a snap, crackle, or pop; when the dog still hasn't learned what it means to be "house broken"; or when some wise person has hidden the remote control from you, we can still rejoice in the fact that this day is a gift from the Lord. We can help those family members around us better understand that the Lord is still in control, helping us to share hope and joy through everyday life.

In case your family is looking for specifics to encourage your "walking and talking and laughing together," here are some further suggestions from some families in which I've been involved.

1   Put up a "laugh wall" in your home. Put large pieces of newsprint up each week and encourage family members to draw pictures, write funny lines, or add their favorite joke or story. This is a good way to keep family members focused on love and laughter.

2   Decorate your refrigerator. What "theological statements" does your refrigerator now proclaim? It can be a great place to tape poems, sayings, pictures of kids and pictures from

kids, favorite jokes, and reasons why people should probably not open the refrigerator door too often! After seeing the movie *Mother*, one family put a note on the freezer door that said, "Protective ice on ice cream may be damaging to our health!"

3 Subscribe to *The Joyful Noiseletter*, a newsletter that shares cartoons, stories, and jokes through resurrection eyes. A great buy for $22 from Fellowship of Merry Christians, P. O. Box 895, Portage, MI 49081–0895.

4 Have fun with your message on the answering machine. Down with boring messages! As a family, develop your own creative ways to tell folks you are not home or you would rather not talk to anyone at this time.

5 Invest in Post-it notes. Leave these little self-sticking notes on the bathroom mirror, on the front door, and even on your spouse's pillow at night. A great way to say "hi" and "I love you."

6 Share Scripture regularly. During family prayers, bedtime talks with the Lord and with family members, keep your home humming with the sound of God's Word.

7 Invite friendly people over to connect with your family. Joy and happiness in the Lord is contagious. Work at helping your family members rub shoulders with other children, youth, and adults who are good models of living out a joy-filled life in Christ.

8 Record cassette tapes to share with a grandparent many miles away, send a video to a family member out of town, use the telephone to keep connected with family members living many miles away from you. Regularly communicating your joys and hopes with others goes a long way to make "uneventful events" significant learning points in a person's life.

9 Write down the stories you hear from family members. Every family has enough material to write a book about themselves. Encourage children, youth, and adults to keep a diary, or at least a journal, that records both the Easter stories and the Good Friday stories in their daily lives. Revisit these pages each week to reflect on the joys, the blessings, and the challenges the Lord continues to give to you and your family.

10 Take pictures! As Hazel always says, "Life is a photo op!" Invest in film and take lots of pictures not only during special holidays, but also capture family members just doing nothing. It's a great opportunity to laugh and share the joys of the people around you whom you love so much.

If you tied buttered toast to the back of a cat and dropped him, what would happen?

Think of other activities you have done or could do as a family. Share these thoughts with other families so they can enjoy your experiences as well. Look for the ho-ho-hos in your home. Blurt out the har-har-hars of your heart. See laughter as "internal jogging." Get good exercise each day. Children, youth, and adults do teach each other the joys of living in the Lord. Continue to be a teacher and a learner. A favorite quote in my family as I was growing up was, "I got my sense of humor from my mother—that's why she doesn't have one anymore!" (But I do think she still is laughing!) Enjoy this day as we teach and talk and sit and walk and lie down and write down the joys and hopes that are ours because Christ has certainly brought the ho-hos and ha-has of life into our homes and hearts!

Before they invented drawing boards, what did they go back to?

GRANDPARENTiNG iS "GRAND"!

One of God's greatest gifts to people is grandchildren! They give us hope, joy, satisfaction, and a sign of God's presence in our lives.

Grandparents have much to offer. We can serve as the "middle people" between our grandkids and their parents. As one parent recently said, "I know my kids are growing up because they have stopped asking me where they came from and now refuse to tell me where they are going!" That's not always the case for grandparents. Grandparents are good at listening, sorting out differing views, and telling faith stories of how the Lord loves and forgives all of us.

A WHAT-To-Do-LiST

Here are some "tried and true" activities for grandparents.

* Keep family traditions alive and well. Remember each others' baptismal dates. Make birthday cakes for one another. Send "love notes" to each other on special occasions.

* Let them know you love them. Hug them, make strong eye-to-eye contact each time you

see them, spend special alone time with each grandchild through special outings, lunches, visits to school, or just plain "doing nothing" on a certain day.

* "Long-distance" grandparenting works also. Use both old and new ways of communicating with each other. Share homemade videos, phone regularly, use e-mail, pray for each other, send photographs, clip news articles of special interest, or send a special gift for no reason at all.

* Work hard at listening and talking to each other. Ask your grandkids for their advice and opinions. Don't ask only "How are you doing in school?" but ask also about their own joys and struggles.

Has anyone actually seen the movie, "Closed for the Season"?

BE "CRAZY" ABOUT GRANDKIDS

Remember that we are the grandparents and not the parents. One of our best roles is to help spoil our grandkids. It is just as proper for grandparents to spoil their grandchildren as it is improper for parents to do so. Every child needs to know that there is at least one adult in the world that "is crazy about me." Work hard at being this "crazy" person to your grandchild!

And as we talk and listen and hug and smile and forgive each other, we also tell our "faith stories" to each other about God's love for us in Jesus Christ. God provides opportunities for us to bring hope to our grandkids, and amazingly enough, as we share our hope in Jesus Christ with them, they are able to share their hope in Jesus Christ with us! That's what I call ministry!

Yes, it's grand to be grandparents! Enjoy your life with them, and your lives together in the Lord!

What kind of sound does
a writing instrument make?

i CAN'T SEE THE DARK!

My friend Aaron was having trouble going to sleep one night. As a 2-year-old, he was usually very good about saying his prayers and heading for bed. But tonight was different. He decided to crawl in bed with his grandfather, who was leisurely reading in the bedroom. What a nice "feel good" way of getting to sleep. But as Aaron tried to sleep, he just couldn't doze off to the land of the z-z-z-z-z's. Something was not quite right.

Then Aaron's father came in to check on his young son. "Aaron, it's time to go to sleep. Say goodnight to Grandpa and close your eyes."

And then Aaron spoke one of his "famous" statements: "Grandpa left the light on, and I can't see the dark!"

How profound! Because of the light I was using while reading, Aaron's routine was disturbed. He couldn't see the dark!

Oh, people of faith, wouldn't it be wonderful if we could protect all children everywhere so they could not see all of the darkness around them? The pain, sorrow, destruction, anger, and all of the other sins? Wouldn't it be perfect if we could guard them against all the sin that is part of their lives and ours? If only we could stop children from seeing and experiencing the darkness of the real world.

Aaron, and other children, we adults do wish we could stop you from seeing the dark. But to no avail. The darkness of sin and death is upon us. Perhaps, instead, we can assist and support you so as you see the darknesses of life, you will also see the "lightnesses" of life, beginning with Christ Jesus.

Aaron, and others, look to the Light of lights, Jesus Christ, as your source of comfort and hope. And in the midst of the darknesses of life, always know that Christ, the Light, is there, overcoming the darkness. John 8:12 says it well: "When Jesus spoke again to the people, He said, 'I am the light of the world. Whoever follows Me will never walk in darkness, but will have the light of life.'"

Aaron, thanks for helping us to deal with the darkness in our lives. When we see that darkness surrounding us, help others to also sense the light of Christ, which comes to overpower the darkness.

Sleep well, little friend. Even when you do see the darkness, be assured that the Light of Christ is always with you!

Shouldn't airports be called something other than "terminals"?

40

WHAT'S TAKEN SO LONG?

Listen to this significant quote from none other than Dr. Martin Luther himself: "Our physical health depends in large measure on the thoughts of our minds ... This is in accord with the saying, 'Good cheer is half the battle.'"

What is especially revealing in these words is that Luther wrote them in a letter to Conrad Cordatus in the year 1537.

What has taken us, the church, so long to catch on? Luther knew all along that there was a direct link between our minds and our bodies. Instead of merging these parts of ourselves, we have argued for years over where the mind, heart, body, and even the soul fit together—if at all.

It is most encouraging to sense a strong renewal in congregations and in personal lives regarding health and wholeness. We used to talk about church growth, which is always a stimulating discussion in itself. Now we tend to talk more about church health.

This can be a positive blessing to all of us, as long

as we continue to strongly emphasize that it is the Lord who provides health, healing, and wholeness to His church and not any specific program, staff position, strategy, or vision for the church. These can all be instruments through which the Lord works, but never an end in themselves.

Thank the Lord for Martin Luther. Right on target, as usual! And let's continue to speak out and write letters and advocate a ministry of healing, hope, and wholeness, all in the name of the healing Christ!

Have you ever experienced amnesia
and deja vu at the same time?

i WiSH i HAD SAiD THAT!

We all hear cute slogans, clever quips, and scintillating stories every day. Some I remember. Some I try to forget. Some I wish I could recall.

Following are a number of such quotes that I've heard in the past few days. Maybe you can fit them into your next conversation, discussion, family devotion, or just idle talk around the coffee bar on Sunday morning. And let me suggest that if you are hearing much better stories and quips than I am, please feel free to share your gems with me.

I find it fascinating to look at a quote or saying from someone else and build a story, article, or message around it, surrounded by Law and Gospel. Some of these fit right in. Others you may have to "stretch" a bit.

1 Robert Orben once said: "I want to thank and pay tribute to all of our volunteers—those dedicated people who believe in all work and no pay."

2 Mother Teresa is quoted as saying: "True holiness consists in doing God's will with a smile."

3 *Seen on a refrigerator door:*

If you sleep on it, make it up.
If you wear it, hang it up.
If you drop it, pick it up.
If you eat out of it, wash it.
If you open it, close it.
If you turn it on, turn it off.
If you empty it, fill it up.
If it rings, answer it.
If it howls, feed it.
If it cries, love it!

4 Heather Whitestone is credited with this one-liner: "The most handicapped person in the world is a negative thinker."

5 Leon Bloy says: "Joy is the most infallible sign of the presence of God."

6 Some good words from Robert K. Greenleaf and the Servant Leadership Center in Indianapolis: "Not much happens without a dream. And for something great to happen, there must be a great dream. Behind every great achievement is a dreamer of great dreams. Much more than a dreamer is required to bring it to reality, but the dream must be there first."

7 One of my favorites: "The perception of a problem is always relative. Your headache feels terrific to the druggist."

8 And another one from the oft-quoted prophet, Anonymous: "Enough about me. Now, let's talk about you. Tell me, what do you think about me?"

9 Words to live by: "It is salutary if we do this—it diminishes us if we do not. It is useful if we do this—it is detrimental if we do not."

10 And for you statistical buffs out there: "Three statisticians go deer hunting with bows and arrows. They spot a big buck and take aim. One shoots and his arrow hits ten feet to the left. The second shoots and his arrow hits ten feet to the right. The third statistician jumps up and down yelling, "We got him! We got him!"

11 From an Australian Aborigine woman: "If you come to help me, then you can go home again. But if you see my struggle as part of your own survival, then perhaps we can work together."

12 Something I wish I would have said: "A keen sense of humor helps us to overlook the unbecoming, understand the unconventional, tolerate the unpleasant, overcome the unexpected, and outlast the unbearable."

What if there were no hypothetical questions?!

As we listen and share these quips and quotes, we also continue to focus on the Scriptures that bring so much wealth and health to us as we continue our ministries together. We continue to listen intently to Scripture each Sunday. We continue to share God's Word through individual family devotions. And we continue to sense the presence of the Spirit in us and bring before the Lord the prayer of King Solomon, "Lord, give me a listening heart."

Blessings and joy as you share these quips and quotes and, above all, as we share the stories of Jesus' love and forgiveness of each of us. Now that's really something to share!

If all the world's a stage,
where is the audience sitting?

AFFIRMING THOSE AROUND US

We often take for granted those servants of the Lord who surround us each day with joy and hope. Some of these people are the workers in our congregations. Why not spend some time this week praying for them? You might also wish to send them a note of appreciation, or call them, have lunch, or offer to baby-sit their kids; or even send them a singing telegram.

You may also want to develop your own "Top 10" list of special words of affirmation that you and others can share with your church staff. Here is the start of such a list.

How many illegal secretaries are there?

PROFESSIONAL CHURCH WORKERS
TOP 10 LIST

What pastors and others would like to hear from laypersons!

10 Hey, it's my turn to sit in the front pew!

9 I was so enthralled, I never noticed the sermon went over by 20 minutes!

8 Personally, I find witnessing more enjoyable than golf.

7 Pastor, I've decided to give our church the $500 a month that I have been sending to the TV evangelist.

6 I volunteer to permanently serve as the Sunday school teacher for the junior high class.

5 Forget the denominational guidelines; let's pay our church staff a living wage!

4 I love it when we sing hymns we've never sung before.

3 Since we're all here, let's start the worship service early.

2 Pastor, we'd like to send you to that Bible seminar in the Bahamas.

1 Nothing inspires me and strengthens my commitment like the annual church business meeting.

(Adapted from various sources)

43

JUST FOR FUN

Sometimes it is good for the soul to have a chance to really laugh—and laugh out loud. Forget what people will think or say. Who cares? Laughter is a gift to use and use again. And it is a gift that keeps on giving.

The following is one of the funnier stories that is a favorite with young children, though some of us "oldies" still chuckle at it also.

Read it and laugh. Share it and laugh. And don't even think of trying to find some theological significance in it—just enjoy it for what it is!

A young man has spent five years traveling throughout the world making a documentary on native dances. He is nearing the end of his project and winds up in Australia in Alice Springs. He begins to talk to an Aborigine, who asks the researcher if he ever saw the "Butcher Dance."

"Butcher Dance? What's that?" he asks.

"What? You no see the Butcher Dance?"

"No, I've never heard of it."

Well, the Aborigine convinces the fellow that he must see the "Butcher Dance" to finish his project. Once convinced, the man gets excited about being able to experience this very famous dance. They begin their trek over the outback to a place where the Butcher Dance is observed. They follow a dirt track for 200 miles, walking for three days through creeks and valleys. It takes them another four days to get over the mountains. And all this time they, of course, are dragging their camera equipment and crew with them.

After seven long days of grueling travel, they finally reach the village of the Butcher Dance. They find the village chief and explain to him why they have travelled so far and say they are anxious to start filming this exotic dance.

Then the bad news hits them. The chief explains that the Butcher Dance Festival was the previous night. The chief adds, "Maybe you can see it the next time."

"Well, when will you hold the next dance?" the researcher asks.

"Not 'til next year."

"Couldn't you please hold it just one more time tonight so we could see it and film it for our documentary?"

"No," was the reply. "The Butcher Dance is very holy and is performed only once a year."

The man is devastated but has no other option than to wait until next year. So he decides to stay in the area and tries to make a go of it in the village, even though it is very difficult. He becomes ill, cannot find work, misses his family, but alas, he sticks it out.

A year passes and the day of reckoning comes—
the next festival of the Butcher Dance. The natives
form a circle around a huge roaring fire. A deathly
hush descends over the performers and some sort of
witch doctor appears and begins the ritual. The
researcher is getting caught up in the fervor of the
event. Wow, *he thinks,* here I am, the first white
man to see the famous Butcher Dance. *He starts*
filming. The chief strides to his position in the circle
and, in a big booming voice, starts to sing. He says,
"You butch yer right arm in. You butch yer right
arm out. You butch yer right arm in and you shake
it all about!"

My uncle reads the obits every day.
He can't understand how people
always die in alphabetical order.

EASTER JOY TURNS THE WORLD UPSIDE DOWN!

"The victory is ours!" shout the people of God. Easter has turned the world upside down! Christ's resurrection is all it took!

And now we are called to bring a real joy into our world. Not a joy in earthly things only, but first and foremost a joy in Christ that leads us to a real celebration around water and Word.

The joy and laughter we are talking about does not come because the best team just won the NBA finals; or we just won the lottery; or we just got that promotion, or award, or test grade; or we get to take the vacation trip we've been working for. These all are things for which to be thankful, but nothing replaces where the real joy and laughter comes from—Christ Himself!

So we are called to bring this victory theme into a world that often does not understand. It does not understand that we can chant, "We're number 2," or 10, or whatever because it really does not matter. For we know we are all "number 1" in God's eyes.

We are called to turn the world upside down. Where there are tears, we bring laughter; where there is war, we bring peace; where there is strife, we bring harmony; where there is hopelessness, we bring hope.

It reminds me of the Pepper and Salt Association, which recently released a campaign to turn the English language around, or "outside in," as they say. It wants phrases changed—for instance, kaboodle and kit. People should listen to roll 'n' rock, eat butter and bread, and travel fro and to. Why? Because what this country needs is a sense of fair play and justice, order and law. There are cons and pros, but true believers will consider it a matter of death and life, a swim or sink proposition!

Let's continue to turn the world upside down, beginning with each of us. And let's do it through the Gospel and Law!

Do cruise ships have car control?

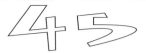

TiME iS CELEBRATiON

How we spend our time is a strong sign of how we celebrate life. How we spend our time also shows our priorities, our hopes, our dreams, our vision for the future.

Here is a story that says it well.

"Daddy, how much do you make an hour?" With a timid voice and idolizing eyes, the little boy greeted his father as he returned from work.

Greatly surprised, but giving his boy a glaring look, the father said, "Look, son, not even your mother knows that. Don't bother me now, I'm tired."

"But, Daddy, just tell me please! How much do you make an hour?" the boy insisted.

The father sighed in frustration. "Twenty dollars per hour."

"Okay, Daddy. Could you loan me 10 dollars?" the boy asked.

Having had enough of his son's questions, the father yelled, "So that was the reason you asked how much I earn, right? Go to sleep and don't bother me anymore!"

Later on, the father was meditating on what he had said and felt rather guilty. Maybe, *he thought,* his son wanted to buy something.

Trying to ease his mind, the father went to his son's room. "Are you asleep, son?" the father asked.

"No, Daddy. Why?" replied the boy, though he really was partially asleep.

"Here's the money you asked for earlier," the father said.

"Thanks, Daddy!" rejoiced the son, putting his hand under his pillow and removing some other money. "Now I have enough! Now I have 20 dollars!" The father just gazed down at him in confusion until his son asked, "Daddy, could you sell me one hour of your time?"

How much do you cost an hour? Every day, every hour, is really a gift. Take time to celebrate your life with someone close to you; continue to give away the gifts of life and time to others!

Why doesn't anyone watch their height?

46

THE GIFT OF TODAY

"This is the day the LORD has made ..." And He's done a pretty good job!

Today is a gift from the Lord. Some of the best models for living life to the fullest are older adults, who continue to emulate what celebrating life is all about. Even though their bodies may not respond as quickly as they used to, or their hearing is not as sharp as years ago, they still see life as a gift from the Lord—for today!

For instance, a 75-year-old man was asked how he felt one morning. He quickly replied, "Amazed!" Or a clever little grandma who needed a hearing aid kept saying to her well-meaning family, "No, at my age I've heard everything I want to hear!" Then there's the grandmother who started dating a 93-year-old man. They never argue—they can't hear each other!

Here is a poem by an anonymous author who captured the joy and excitement of life each day.

*Today, Dear Lord, I'm 80, and
there's much I haven't done.
I hope, dear Lord, You'll let me live
until I'm 81.*

*But then, if I haven't finished
all I want to do,
Would You let me stay awhile—
until I'm 82?*

125

So many places I want to go,
so very much to see—
Do You think that You could manage
to make it 83?

The world is changing very fast,
there is so much in store—
I'd like it very much to live
until I'm 84.

And if by then I'm still alive,
I'd like to stay till 85.

More planes will be up in the air,
so I'd really like to stick—
And see what happens to the world
when I'm 86.

I know, dear Lord, it's much to ask
(and it must be nice in heaven),
But I would really like to stay
until I'm 87.

I know by then I won't be fast
and sometimes will be late,
But it would be so pleasant—
to be around at 88.

I will have seen so many things,
and had a wonderful time.
So I'm sure that I'll be willing
to leave at 89 … Maybe!

RISE ... AND WHINE!

I have a friend who insists that her spouse just never gets anything right. And to top it off, he doesn't even "rise and shine." Instead, he rises ... and whines!

There is a lot of that going around these days. Complain, complain, complain. Nothing ever goes right. The world is going down the tubes!

There is a story about an elderly lady in a nursing home who was always complaining. The food was either too hot or too cold. No one visited her. People were not friendly to her. Her pastor came regularly to see her, though quite reluctantly because he would get depressed just hearing all of her complaints. One day he lost his cool, and as she continued to hammer away at everything that was ever wrong in the world, he heard her ask, "Oh, why doesn't the Lord take me to heaven with Him?"

Without thinking, the pastor blurted out, "Well, maybe He doesn't want you!"

Maybe some of us are still on this earth because the Lord doesn't want us in our current condition of comparing and seeing life as a pain, a problem, and a hopeless situation. In reality, we can rejoice because there is hope in this world. It is spelled C-H-R-I-S-T T-H-E L-O-R-D! The question for us is not "What is this world coming to?" but the exclamation, "Look who's come into this world!" Christ Jesus Himself is alive and working through each of us.

So rejoice, fear not, and celebrate the presence, hope, and peace of the Lord of all life! This is not the type of hope and peace the world gives—empty and short-lived. Rather it is the hope and peace of our Lord, Christ Jesus—living and eternal. And it gives us every reason in the world to rise and ... shine!

Why do power outages always happen at 12:00?

JESUS iS WiTH US

Rachel did not want to go upstairs by herself. "It's too dark up there," she said. "And I'm afraid." Grandpa, trying to comfort her and teach her at the same time, commented, "But do you know who else is up there with you?"

"Yes, yes, I know, Jesus is—but I want someone up there with me whom I can see!"

Someone whom she could see. How powerful a response! How thoughtful! How real! How theological!

Seven-year-old Rachel taught Grandpa a significant lesson that night. Sure, Jesus is with us always (even to the "end of the age"), but how important it is that we as God's people become "Jesus with skin on" to those around us. And for that fleeting moment of walking up the stairs with Rachel, Grandpa was "Jesus with skin on" to her.

And Rachel will be that "Jesus with skin on" person to people in her life also, as she listens to friends, hugs her parents, speaks well of her teachers, and commits her life to service to others in the name of Jesus.

To whom can you bring a word of hope today? Who needs to "see" Jesus in his or her life? How can you reach out to touch this person? Whom will the Lord put in your life this week that is also afraid of the darkness of the world?

We as God's celebrating people bring Christ the Light to this darkened world. We affirm the Spirit at work, we celebrate life as a gift, we see the actions of God through the news events of the day, and we help people see and interpret the Spirit at work in their lives.

The Lord is with us! The Lord is with others! Let us sing "What a Friend We Have in Jesus," but let us also sing, "What a Jesus We Have in Friends"!

Do they have coffee breaks at the Lipton Tea Company?

CELEBRATING LIFE

When we speak about celebration, we often talk only of the happy, pleasant, fun times of our lives. Celebration comes to mean only that feeling when we can forget about our problems and pains and totally immerse ourselves in music and dance and laughter and fun times.

But that is not what God has in mind for us celebrating people! Celebration is only possible through the deep realization that life and death are never completely separated. Real celebration, in Christ, is only found when joy and sorrow, laughter and tears, fear and love exist together. As Henri Nouwen states: "Celebration is the acceptance of life in a constantly increasing awareness of its preciousness.

Do archaeologists listen to rock music?

And life is precious not only because it can be touched, seen, and tasted, but also because it will be gone one day."

There are tears at weddings and smiles at funerals. For life and death are not opponents, but they are teammates at every moment of life. In *Creative Ministry*, our friend Henri shares the following:

"When we are born we become free to breathe on our own but lose the safety of our mother's body; when we go to school we are free to join a greater society but lose a particular place in our family; when we marry we find a new partner but lose the special tie we had with our parents; when we find work we win our independence by making our own money but lose the stimulation of teachers and fellow students; when we receive children we discover a new world but lose much of our freedom to move; when we are promoted we become more important in the eyes of others but lose the chance to take many risks; when we retire we finally have the chance to do what we want but lose the support of being wanted." [9]

Why is "easy listening" music so hard to listen to?

When we are able to celebrate life through all our pains and sorrows, joys, and hoorays, throughout gaining and losing in life, we have finally learned how to celebrate real life in Christ. Then, as Matthew 16:25 points out, "For whoever wants to save his life will lose it, but whoever loses his life for Me, will find it." We will then be able to celebrate even in death. For dying in Christ means we receive real life. And what a real and eternal celebration that will be!

50

A QUIET JOY

All of our joy and celebration does not come in loud gushes of laughter and blasts of trumpets. There is also a "quiet joy," which the Spirit brings to us. It is the awareness that the Lord is indeed with us. It is knowing Psalm 46:10 backward and forward: "Be still and know that I am God." It is knowing that even when we are alone, we aren't.

This quiet joy from God isn't always readily apparent. In fact, we usually need to set aside time to be alone with God to feel it. Getting away from the phones, the television, our work, and even our loved ones is most difficult, to say the least. These people and callings are our life!

But the Lord says to us, "When you pray, go into your room, close the door, and pray …" (Matthew 6:6). Do this so you can hear the quietness of God's joy descending on you and working in your heart.

It is this quiet joy—a true gift from God—that can speak to us so powerfully, especially in trials and struggles. Work at finding those quiet times in your life—without TV, radio, the chaos that surrounds us—and listen to the presence and power of the Lord.

Thanks, Lord, for the "quiet joy" in our lives. Thanks for the times to be healed and touched by You so we are empowered and enabled to touch and heal others in Your name!

CHILDREN AND ADULTS—TOGETHER

A little boy said to his Sunday school teacher one day, "Hey, there's something I can't figger out."

"What's that, Billy?" asked the teacher.

"Well, accordin' to the Bible, the children of Israel crossed the Red Sea, right?"

"Right."

"An' the children of Israel beat up the Philistines, right?"

"Er—right."

"An' the children of Israel built the temple, right?"

"Again you're right."

"An' the children of Israel fought the 'Gyptians, an' the children of Israel fought the Romans, an' the children of Israel wuz always doin' somethin' important, right?"

"All that is right too," his teacher agreed. "So what's your question?"

"What I wanna know is this," demanded Billy. "What wuz all the grown-ups doin'?"

What were all the grown-ups doing? What a powerful question from little Billy, a special person of God.

Well, grown-ups, what are we doing in terms of sharing our faith and joys with others? Billy is right.

Often we adults are not as visible and verbal as we should be. We do have a lot of teaching and listening and mentoring to do in this world.

For starters, take a look at all the children and youth in our lives. Beautiful people of God! These playful kids continue to tell us about love and life in ways that no books ever did. They help us realize that only when we enter into their joys will we also be able to enter into their pain and struggles. It seems that the Lord is pushing all of us to walk into the world with a little child on each hand—to comfort, guide, learn, and celebrate together.

Watch for the children in your lives. Celebrate with them. Spend time with them. Tell the story of Jesus to them. Read to them. Hug them.

Then when someone asks, "Where are all the grown-ups?" we can proudly say, "We are playing with the children!"

Why don't health cereals
have free prizes in them?

GUiDELiNES FOR CELEBRATING THE CHRiST-LiFE

Care more than you think is wise;
Risk more than you think is safe;
Dream more than you think is practical;
Expect more than you think is possible;
Celebrate more than you think is necessary;
Comfort more than you think is comfortable;
Forgive more than you think is called for;
Hope more than you think is appropriate;
Live in the joy of the Lord!

WELL NOW!

"Well now!" is a strong phrase that invites us to see that all of our wellness comes from the Lord. "Well now!" is a statement of faith in Christ Jesus that He and He alone brings health and healing to the world and also to us.

"Well now!" Isn't that good news? You bet it is! For we are called by God to live "well now!" lives by first of all realizing that wellness is a gift from God to all people.

The invitation to be "well now!" is an invitation to revel in the goodness of God; live in freedom and responsibility; enjoy the gifts of food, drink, rest, exercise, companionship, time alone, relaxation, confession, forgiveness, anticipation of the future, and the full rich joy of the moment. "Well now!" is not a mandate from the Lord to get our act together or else! Instead, "Well now!" is an affirmation of God's power and will for us to live healthy and whole lives as His special creations on this earth.

"Well now!" Yes, we are in Christ Jesus as He continues to love and forgive us and make us well!

A FINAL WORD ON— LET THERE BE LAUGHTER!

Let There Be Laughter is a positive mind-set toward life. It is not only something we do, it is something we are. We do not manufacture or create or even make possible this gift of laughter—it is from God. And we can laugh with Him as the Giver of this gift.

Jesus says in John 15:11–12: "I have told you this so that My joy may be in you and that your joy may be complete. My command is this: Love each other as I have loved you. Greater love has no one than this, that he lay down his life for his friends."

Let There Be Laughter is about loving others the way Christ first loved us—by giving ourselves and our lives to those around us. Our lives become "laughable lives" as the Spirit moves in and through us with His unconditional love.

Laughter and joy and celebration are all wrapped up into lives of commitment and service to others. Our health and healing come about as Christ ministers to us through others. So we continue the celebration that started that first Easter day. The laughter has only just begun!

Have a *Let There Be Laughter* type of day—and life!

SARAH'S CHRISTMAS SCENARIO -1998-

(Bimler Grandchild #5)

Hi! My name is SARAH RUTH CILLICK. I'm 4 months old, and I'm happy to write you this greeting. People already say that I have better handwriting than my GRANDPA, but that's not saying much, I guess.

Let me tell you about my new family. ... As you can see from the photo, I'm the cutest one of them all, but they are all nice to me, most of the time, except when GRANDMA keeps wanting me to look at all of her photos! That's why I sleep most of the time!

GRANDMA and GRANDPA (their real names are RICH and HAZEL, but I don't know why they get two names) seem to have fun together. They traveled to China this fall, right after I was born (I hope it had nothing to do with me!). They really liked the people, and, even though they didn't get to see the Great Wall, they said they enjoyed seeing the "pretty nice" wall. GRAMS brought a shirt back that read, "Rice is my life." I really didn't understand it, but I've already learned to just laugh and smile! ... GRAMS and GRAMPS wrote a new book together called *A Word to My Sponsor* (CPH, 1998), which I already gave to my Baptism godparents. They say it's good, but there's too

139

many big words in it for me!

GRAMPS continues to enjoy WHEAT RIDGE MINISTRIES and hopes everyone continues to support it too. (HE told me to say this!) ... GRAMS had some health problems this year, and her theme song is "Avoid Your Thyroid." GRAMPS was sick too, and when the insurance wouldn't cover one of his ailments, the doctor was nice enough to touch up the x-rays. ... I still think GRAMPS drinks too much Starbucks coffee. He always tells people, "Thanks a Latte!"

DIANE and MARTY, my parents, are really great. I wake them up often, just to tell them. ... They keep busy doing lots of things at church, school, and in shopping malls. After I was born, MOM went on a diet of coconuts and bananas. She hasn't lost weight, but she can sure climb trees! ... **MATT,** my 9-year-old brother, is the best brother I got. He reads, teases his sisters, plays basketball, teases his sisters. He even showed me his baseball cards once. He knew I couldn't read yet, so he told me to just look at the pitchers. ... **RACHEL** is my 7-year-old sis. She's lots of fun, except when she thinks I'm a Beanie Baby. She's already teaching me how to get a brother in trouble! ... **HANNAH,** 3, takes real good care of me, like making sure I don't sleep too long. She even calls me "Barbie" as she stretches and turns my arms and legs around and around. But I love her anyway! ... My DAD is finishing our basement. It's going to be a "best cellar"!

And I even have more family! My uncle **BOB** calls me "Baby Ruth." He's like that a lot. He lives somewhere near here where they drive fast. Oh yeah, Inianapplesauce, or something like that. BOB and GRAMPS wrote a book together, which I hope will be published by the time I can read. It's called *Let There Be Laughter!* (CPH, 1999). Watch for it. BOB enjoys sports, except for tackle football 'cause he broke his "pinkie." And he was just watching a Colts game on TV! He's still single and has found out that the best way to impress a young lady at the gym is to do pull-ups—pull up in a Corvette, pull up in a Rolls Royce. (I don't get this either, but GRAMPS thought it would work.) I sure love big Uncle BOB! ...

MIKE, JILL, and AARON are my uncle, aunt, and cousin (in that order, I think). They live in St. Louis, which is a long-g-g-g way from Chicago according to GRAMS. I like Mike! He's a therapist, and all I know about that is that people say he sure has a lot of work to do with his own relatives. JILL is so nice too. And clever. MIKE asked once what she did with AARON all day. JILL reminded MIKE that a mother works from son up to son down! AARON is 3, going on 18. He's a big guy, so big that this year Santa wanted to sit on his lap! ... UNCLE MIKE broke his leg skiing. Our family has had a lot of breaks this year.

SARAH, that's me, is so happy to join this friendly family. I think we'll have lots of great times together. And, as my GRANDPARENTS say, that's because we have so many super friends around us—like YOU, I bet! I can't wait to meet YOU! I like YOU already!

Thanks for listening. I'm going shopping with GRAMS now. She buys anything marked down, so I think we're going to buy an escalator. And isn't it romantic how GRAMS and GRAMPS always hold hands together? I thought so too until I found out that if he lets go, she goes shopping.

I'm so glad to be born into this family, especially

so I can celebrate the birth of another baby, Jesus, who brings health and hope and healing to all of us, young and old, each day. That's the bestest part of Christmas anyway! I'm all for that.

Blessed Christmas! Come visit my GRAMS and GRAMPS. You could even sleep in my crib. There's always room in the Bim Inn.

RICH and HAZEL

(with thanks to SARAH and the whole family)

NOTE: Even though this letter is not Y2K compatible, we are happy to report that the BIMLER family is compatible, at least most of the time!

Warning: Humor may be hazardous to your illness!

12 WARNING SIGNS OF HEALTH

1 Persistent presence of supportive friends
2 Chronic positive expectations—a tendency to frame events in a positive light
3 Regular signs of joy in living
4 Sense of spiritual renewal in the Lord
5 Increased sensitivity to others
6 A tendency to adapt to changing conditions
7 Increased appetite for physical activity
8 Tendency to identify and communicate feelings
9 Repeated episodes of gratitude and generosity
10 Compulsion to care for other people
11 Persistent sense of humor; known to laugh out loud
12 A life centered in the forgiveness of Christ!

*May the God of hope fill you with all joy and peace
as you trust in Him so that you may overflow
with hope by the power of the Holy Spirit.*
Romans 15:13

From: Wheat Ridge Ministries
1 Pierce Place, Suite 250E
Itasca, IL 60143-2634
(800) 762-6748
http://www.wheatridge.org

ENDNOTES

1 Leigh Ann Jasheway, *Don't Get Mad—Get Funny! Using Humor to Manage Stress: A Light-Hearted Approach to Stress Management,* (Whole Person Associates, 1996).

2 Allen Klein, *The Healing Power of Humor,* (New York, New York: Jeremy P. Tarcher, Inc., 1989).

3 Dr. August Mennicke. Used by permission.

4 Lois Peacock, Editor, "Bay Area Health Ministries" newsletter, Summer 1997.

5 Valerie Bell, *Getting Out of Your Kids' Faces* (Grand Rapids, Michigan: Zondervan Publishing House, 1994). Used by permission.

6 Richard Bimler, *Pray, Praise and Hooray,* (St. Louis, Missouri: Concordia Publishing House, 1972). Used by permission.

7 C. S. Lewis, *The Screwtape Letters,* (Hammersmith, London: HarperCollins Publishers). Used by permission.

8 Robert Coles, *The Moral Intelligence of Children,* (New York, New York: Random House, 1997).

9 Henri J. M. Nouwen, *Creative Ministry,* (New York, New York: Doubleday, 1991). Used by permission.